Lost in Work

'A brilliant, searing exposé of the lies underpinning work.'

—Owen Jones

'Fascinating and absorbing ... a corrective to the widespread view that anyone can find fulfilment through their job, if they just work hard enough.'

—Grace Blakeley, editor of *Futures of Socialism*

'Amelia Horgan is, in the words of organiser Fred Ross, a social arsonist. Her book will set your world on fire. Somewhere in our bones, we know that work is getting worse. But with this book, Horgan has provided the match and the kindling we need to burn the whole thing down.'

—Sarah Jaffe, author of *Work Won't Love You Back*

'At last, a book that helps us appreciate the long history of the working-class challenge to the tyranny of work that puts class struggle in the workplace firmly back on the agenda.'

—John McDonnell, former Shadow Chancellor of the Labour Party

'An excellent and important book. It combines sharp political insight with nuanced analyses ... an invaluable resource to those with an interest not just in better understanding labour and exploitation, but also in the possibilities of freedom and collective joy.'

—Helen Hester, Professor of Gender, Technology and Cultural Politics, University of West London, author of *Xenofeminism*

'I can't think of a more succinct and elegant expression of what work does to us and, in turn, why it's never been more urgent to shape our work.'

—Will Stronge, Director of Research at Autonomy and author of *Post-Work*

'An incisive analysis of the contemporary crisis of work – and a ringing call to reimagine it.'

—Amia Srinivasan, Chichele Professor of Social and Political Theory at All Souls College, Oxford, and author of *The Right to Sex: Feminism in the Twenty-first Century*

Outspoken by Pluto
Series Editor: Neda Tehrani

Platforming underrepresented voices; intervening in important political issues; revealing powerful histories and giving voice to our experiences; Outspoken by Pluto is a book series unlike any other. Unravelling debates on feminism and class, work and borders, unions and climate justice, this series has the answers to the questions you're asking. These are books that dissent.

Also available:

Mask Off
Masculinity Redefined
JJ Bola

Border Nation
A Story of Migration
Leah Cowan

Behind Closed Doors
Sex Education Transformed
Natalie Fiennes

Feminism, Interrupted
Disrupting Power
Lola Olufemi

Split
Class Divides Uncovered
Ben Tippet

Lost in Work

Escaping Capitalism

Amelia Horgan

PLUTO  PRESS

First published 2021 by Pluto Press
345 Archway Road, London N6 5AA

www.plutobooks.com

British Library Cataloguing in Publication Data
A catalogue record for this book is available from the British Library

ISBN   978 0 7453 4091 3   Paperback
ISBN   978 1 78680 699 4   PDF
ISBN   978 1 78680 700 7   EPUB
ISBN   978 1 78680 701 4   Kindle

This book is printed on paper suitable for recycling and made from
fully managed and sustained forest sources. Logging, pulping and
manufacturing processes are expected to conform to the environmental standards of the country of origin.

Typeset by Stanford DTP Services, Northampton, England

Simultaneously printed in the United Kingdom and United States of
America

Contents

Acknowledgements   vi

Introduction: Work's fantasy   1

1. Work, capitalism and capitalist work   14
2. Contesting 'work'   32
3. The paradox of new work   48
4. What does work do to us as individuals?   66
5. Jobification nation: When play is serious business   82
6. What does work do to society?   98
7. Phantoms and slackers: Resistance at work   114
8. Getting together: Organised labour and the workers'
   dream   127
9. Time off: Resistance to work   145
Conclusion: Getting to work   161

Acknowledgements

While writing this book, I became very ill. After having Covid-19 in March 2020, I spent most of that year in bed, too weak to get up, struggling to think, and struggling to write. This period of illness meant that this book could only be written in fits and spurts; a few sentences one day, a paragraph or so the next. This means that this is a slightly different book than the book I had imagined it would be. Despite this, I hope it lives up to the promise of theory, of what theory can and *should* do – take what is assumed to be natural, fixed, insurmountable and show it as contingent, mutable, and surmountable. In short, that most fundamental prerequisite for action, hope. Hope for better work, hope against work as we know it, hope for a better world.

When I was ill, I saw quite how much people wanted to care for each other and how much those desires for care were frustrated by the way our society is set up. After an initial (and impressive) flurry of mutual aid activity, older patterns established themselves. Rather than collective, transformative effort, the continuance of day-to-day life was secured through unpaid women's work in the home, and by poorly paid service and logistics work outside of it; the more things change, the more they stay the same. We might be wary of making claims about what people are fundamentally like, but it is striking how much effort is required to interrupt the kindness and care that people desperately want to share with each other.

With that in mind, thanks are due to those friends and comrades who supported me with so much care, and in particular

ACKNOWLEDGEMENTS

to Gabriel (Constantin) Mehmel, Hareem Ghani, Huda Elmi, Martha Perotto-Wills, Jenny Killin and Sean O'Neill.

Special thanks are due to those who read, commented on and vastly improved drafts of chapters: Daisy Porter, Freddie Seale, James Elliott, James Greig, Josh Gabert-Doyon, Orlando Lazar, Neha Shah, Robert Maisey, Sarra Facey, Sam Dolbear, Steffan Blayney and particularly to Lorna Finlayson. Any errors or omissions are my own.

Thanks too to Neda Tehrani for patience and care in editing and support throughout the process of writing this book.

And, to Richard, thank you for everything.

Introduction: Work's fantasy

There's a comforting narrative of progress about work: the bad old days of horrible jobs – of children working in mines, of cotton mills, of workplace injuries, of cruel bosses – are gone. Instead, the only problem of work that we have left is that not everyone has the right kind of job for them, or that barriers prevent particular groups – women, people of colour, disabled people – from accessing particular kinds of jobs. For many, though, the reality of contemporary work is rather different. Against this narrative of progress, we might first point to the continued existence of hazardous work around the world. While most of the extremely dangerous and hyper-exploitative work in extractive industries has been exported to the Global South, in the Global North there are persistent problems of ill health and poor conditions associated with work, and many examples of tyrannical bosses exercising arbitrary power over their employees. In Britain, there were at least 1.4 million workers suffering from work-related ill health in 2018/19.[1] While the number of people who become ill because of work had been decreasing for many years, it briefly increased in the wake of the 2008 financial crisis and has plateaued since.

The Covid-19 crisis has shown that risk of harm to health at work is not evenly distributed. While the lack of PPE, long hours, and offensively low pay that NHS workers faced

---

1 https://hse.gov.uk/statistics/causdis/index.htm (last accessed December 2020).

received rightful condemnation, the risks faced by workers in the low-pay and low-protection service sector were less often remarked upon.[2] Partly, this was because of something of a cover-up by employers: thanks to a loophole that allowed them not to report cases that were, on their judgement, transmitted within the community rather than at work, employers were in practice able to decide for themselves if cases of Covid-19 in their workplace were reported as such.[3] This was a particular problem in the food processing sector, where media reports found at least 1461 cases of Covid-19 and six deaths, yet official reports only declared 47 cases and not a single fatality.[4] At one food processing plant, secret filming revealed that workers were threatened with redundancy for taking sick leave. Similarly, in call centres, workers were expected to continue coming into work, even as other workplaces closed their doors, and even for work that was not 'essential', like debt collection or selling new phone deals.[5] *Essential*, perhaps, not to collective survival in the face of a dangerous new virus, but to profits.

The first stage of the crisis has shown that workers are exposed to very different levels of risk; some of us have been able to work from home, uncomfortable and difficult as that can sometimes be, while others have had no choice but to risk exposure to a potentially deadly virus. Despite the rhetoric about 'essential

2   Even the company that couriered the medical swabs used to test for Covid-19 came under fire for its poor treatment of employees. See https://news.sky.com/story/coronavirus-major-uk-testing-company-broke-health-and-safety-laws-at-height-of-pandemic-12087248 (last accessed December 2020).

3   www.pirc.co.uk/wp-content/uploads/2020/09/PIRC_sector_food_processing.pdf (last accessed December 2020).

4   Ibid.

5   For example, EE call centre workers in Darlington were pressured back to work in March 2020: https://thenorthernecho.co.uk/news/local/darlington/18341404.coronavirus-please-help-us-plead-darlington-ee-call-centre-staff-working-pandemic/ (last accessed December 2020).

workers' and 'key workers', those who had to continue to work in person were not only those whose jobs could reasonably be deemed 'essential'. Just over half of people continued going to work. While 'essential' might conjure up images of supermarket shelf-stackers or of nurses and doctors, in reality, apart from the few sectors that were actually shut down, it was up to employers to declare whether their companies did essential work.[6] When shops were reopened, the risk of death for retail assistants rose to 70% higher than average for men and 65% higher for women.[7] The virus, it turns out, does discriminate. In a society that is highly unequal, like the UK, the conditions under which people will experience the same health problem will be vastly different. These differences are not secondary; rather, they can define the likelihood of becoming sick and the severity of the illness itself. Different workers were exposed to different levels of risk and when combined with structural risks, those subject to them were even more likely to become sick, even more likely to die. In particular, the combination of occupational exposure, poverty and racism meant that Black people died of Covid-19 at nearly twice the rate of white people.[8]

Covid-19 called into question the soothing idea of progressively improving work and it revealed the prevalence of bad new work. Those who do not experience the sharp end of this – the wealthy, who do not rely on earnings from paid work in the same way that the working class does, and some people of older generations for whom work, albeit with significant class, gender,

---

6   https://opendemocracy.net/en/oureconomy/dont-buy-the-lockdown-lie-this-is-a-government-of-business-as-usual/ (last accessed December 2020).

7   https://ons.gov.uk/peoplepopulationandcommunity/healthandsocialcare/causesofdeath/bulletins/coronaviruscovid19relateddeathsbyoccupationenglandandwales/deathsregisteredbetween9marchand25may2020 (last accessed December 2020).

8   https://bbc.co.uk/news/uk-52219070 (last accessed December 2020).

racial and regional disparities did not involve, or only temporarily involved, low-pay or low-protection – inhabit a fantasy world, half-waking half-sleeping. In this world, tyrannical bosses, poverty pay, and dismissal for challenging crap conditions are a thing of the past, or at least, something that happens somewhere else. The story this world tells itself goes like this: it's relatively easy to get a job – just hand your CV into somewhere on the high street! – and once you've got one you can rely on it to keep your rent paid. You can trust that it's unlikely that something bad will happen; or that if it does – say, you get sick, or injured at work – you'll be protected, either legally or by the goodwill of your employer. While you might have to slog away for a few years doing something you're not particularly keen on, eventually, the day will come when you're able to do something you actually enjoy, or, at the very least, you'll be paid enough that it doesn't matter.

The reality is that the kind of jobs you might have once been able to get with a sweep of the high street and your printer-warm CVs now have hundreds of people applying for them. We can attribute the persistence of belief in the possibility of finding good – that is, well-paid, secure and fulfilling – work, despite the foreclosure of that possibility, to a few different things. First among those might be that many have been shielded from the reality of the scale and nature of the problem. This is because the economic stagnation that has dominated this century so far has, in the UK, meant a polarisation of the labour market. The middle has fallen out, with middling-paid occupations lost. This leaves poorly paid work, often part-time or involving bogus self-employment (where those who could legally be counted as employees, and receive rights and benefits as employees, are encouraged by companies to register instead as self-employed), at the bottom, while at the top are a growing number of high-paid occupations.[9] This polarisation isn't spread evenly across the UK. In parts of the south of England, and particularly in London, there are very high levels of inequality and labour polarisation that aren't found to the same extent elsewhere.[10] At the same time, the protections historically offered by the welfare state have been either destroyed or eroded by successive governments, from increased conditionality for benefits that were previously universal to cuts to the amount of benefit that can be received, and the loss of public services. But those who have not experienced the new benefits system, or used decaying public services, and have enough seniority in their workplace to have avoided zero-hours or temporary work, or who have retired and left the job market, may well not have any idea how bad it is, how quickly and totally the rug has been pulled out from under people's feet. They will remember, or still live in, a world of what is termed 'standard employment'. This means full-time, open-ended, contract-bound jobs, with the terms of the contract, and of the reciprocal responsibilities of both employer and employee, enforced by trade unions.

Standard employment, however, is something of a historical anomaly. Before the introduction of the legal apparatus defining the terms of employment, fought for and defended by trade unions, the arbitrary power of employers to hire and fire, to determine hours of work and so on was immense. While the majority of workers are in standard employment in the UK, many are locked out of it, and the sectors in which young people, people of colour, migrants and women are more likely

---

9   https://bl.uk/britishlibrary/~/media/bl/global/business-and-management/pdfs/non-secure/w/a/g/wage-inequality-and-employment-polarisation-in-british-cities.pdf (last accessed December 2020).
10   Ibid.

to work tend to be those more likely to use temporary contracts, zero-hours contracts, subcontracting or bogus self-employment.

All of these (increasingly regular) contractual 'irregularities' give more power and flexibility to employers, allowing them to cut costs on things like National Insurance, sick pay or parental leave, and making it easier and cheaper to fire workers. Zero-hours contract or on-demand work offers flexibility, but that flexibility is often more beneficial to employers than to workers. It means that when there's less demand, workers don't get hours scheduled. It also creates a system of control – workers might have obligations outside of work, say, to pick up their children at a certain time – and putting timetabling only in the hands of managers and bosses means that workers who do not meet particular, often impossibly high, targets, or who complain about conditions, are denied a schedule that works for them.[11] Zero-hours contracts are about 6% of contracts in the UK, but in some sectors, admin and support services, and accommodation and food, this rises to around 20%. Companies in construction and in health and social work make disproportionate use of such contracts. While non-standard employment remains less common than standard employment in the UK, in some sectors, it is growing. This means significant numbers of people are locked out of the legal rights afforded to workers and employees. Globally, most work is actually done outside of the formal sector, which means it is not only likely to be non-standard paid employment but is also outside of the legal and taxation frameworks of the state. As the growth of new jobs slows and more jobs are lost, non-standard employment, or any work that falls outside of the formal sector, might become more common.

---

11 See Alex Wood, *Despotism on Demand* (Ithaca, NY: Cornell University Press, 2020).

INTRODUCTION: WORK'S FANTASY

If we look, with clear eyes, at the state of work in the UK – the prevalence of low wages, low protections, the polarisation, the stickiness of wage stagnation – we might think that something desperately needs to change. We might want to call into question the tidy narrative of progress around work outlined at the start of this introduction. But the response from the political establishment to the diminishing availability of well-paid, secure work has profoundly missed the point. The first response, while on the surface not particularly bad in itself, would be over-generously described as a sticking plaster. We might call this the aspiration-deficit model. It argues that people end up trapped in crap jobs because they don't know what they're capable of and, with the right encouragement, will be able to find a fulfilling job. This encouragement can be helpful, especially when it comes to negotiating the complicated terrain of the unwritten, and often indiscernible to the uninitiated, social capital-bound rules of the workplace. Sometimes this becomes a question of supporting people from particular oppressed groups into better paid, secure work. And while the barriers to career advancement or to certain professions for women, for people of colour and for working-class people are often particularly high, what happens to those who do not make it? The system is such that there will always be many more losers than there are winners. Those who are caught in a punitive and cruel benefit system and successive low-paid crap jobs. Aspiration in a world structurally unable to fulfil the aspirations of everyone will leave the unlucky or just those for whatever reason not capable of meeting their aspirations cast adrift. Sometimes this induced aspiration comes with particular training, but this often fails to address the structural issue of the lack of high-quality jobs. Even when the project of adding aspiration works, it can only help a small few; for everyone else, it's a particularly vicious moment of cruelty in which they are made to feel that their failures are their own fault alone.

The second response to the erosion of work-as-we-previously-knew-it is the pathologisation of the unemployed. This is the stick to the carrot of the aspiration model, and in some ways, an extension of it. Within it, worklessness becomes a sickness, to be cured by hard work.[12] We can see it in the ugly suggestion that workers avoiding a dangerous virus were 'addicted to furlough', and as the Health Secretary Matt Hancock suggested, had to be 'weaned off'. We can see it in the routine invocation of a nonsense binary of 'strivers vs skivers', in former Deputy Prime Minister and deputy architect of austerity Nick Clegg's dreary 'alarm clock Britain', Labour MP Rachel Reeves' insistence that her party was not the party of 'people on benefits', or George Osborne's opposition between the 'shift-worker, leaving home in the dark hours of the early morning' and 'their next-door neighbour sleeping off a life on benefits.'[13] Sometimes this rhetoric even breaks out into open advocacy of eugenics, such as when the Tory MP Ben Bradley wrote that those on benefits should be pointed towards vasectomies.[14] Unemployment becomes a dangerous state, a hereditary sickness, but one that is squarely the fault of the individual. Margaret Thatcher reduced the amount of benefits available to claimants, but it was really only under Major and Blair that conditions began to be attached to benefits. Some conditions reduced the number of people who could claim a particular benefit: these eligibility conditions

12 See *The Work Cure* ed. David Frayne (Monmouth: PCCS Books, 2019) for a helpful discussion of this topic.

13 https://theguardian.com/politics/2013/jan/08/strivers-shirkers-language-welfare (last accessed December 2020).

14 https://theguardian.com/politics/2018/jan/16/ben-bradley-under-fire-for-blogpost-urging-jobless-people-to-have-vasectomies (last accessed December 2020).

barred, for example, students from claiming unemployment benefits they had previously been entitled to over the summer holidays. Other conditions applied to the behaviour of claimants: this could mean compulsory unpaid work, or sanctions for missing appointments; in some cases, sanctions can mean losing eligibility for benefits for up to three years.[15] Not only has the safety net of the welfare state been frayed, its use has been massively stigmatised.[16] None of this does very much to get people into work, although schemes in which people work for free are, presumably, a profitable arrangement for employers. As too is the growth of bogus self-employment, which keeps costs down for employers and leaves workers without the protections of direct employment. It helps keep the unemployment statistics down, too. Of course, there's also money to be made for the private companies to which the business of running much of the welfare state has been outsourced, too. The company that currently administers one of the most notorious parts of the punitive welfare apparatus, the fitness-to-work assessments that determine whether someone is eligible for Employment and Support Allowance, are reportedly paid £200 per assessment.[17]

Two kinds of unfreedom

Despite the problem of persistent low wages and growing in-work poverty, it is still claimed by the government that 'work is the best way out of poverty'.[18] Poverty and unemployment

---

15   https://bbc.co.uk/news/uk-46104333 (last accessed December 2020).

16   https://blogs.lse.ac.uk/politicsandpolicy/benefit-sanctions-mental-health/ (last accessed December 2020).

17   https://theguardian.com/society/2016/jan/08/maximus-miss-fitness-to-work-test-targets-despite-spiralling-costs (last accessed December 2020).

18   https://ft.com/content/d50bd4ec-7c87-11e9-81d2-f785092ab560 (last accessed December 2020).

become individual failings rather than unwanted features of the economy. Between the soft, slow-burning punishment of aspiration and the immediate violence of the benefits system, there is a war being waged against the millions trapped in low waged and insecure work. But this isn't just a book about crap jobs,[19] although the extent and sheer misery of them is evidence enough against the narrative of gradually improving work. It's a book about how work under capitalism is bad for all of us. As we've already seen, work simply does not, as it currently exists, *work* for the lowest paid. But, as I argue in the rest of the book, the problem of work under capitalism is not just the problem of crap jobs and of an unfair distribution of access to better ones. Even in work that is more secure, more permanent, and better paid, all kinds of problems for workers emerge. The reason for this is that, by and large, we are not able to choose how we work. At work, we are subject to control by others. Being subject to the power of others might not be always bad, but the particular way in which this control is exercised, and particularly in the context of a relative powerlessness of workers, means it can be extremely harmful. The lack of freedom in the workplace is, in part, the product of a background condition of work. This background condition is that the majority of society must find a job to be able to live. In this sense, we do not make a free choice to enter work. Of course, we are not forced to work. We are not dragged from our beds and plonked in an office chair, made to look at spreadsheets at gunpoint, and shot if we fail to meet monthly targets – but the kind of society we live in is one in which having a job is a *necessity*. Without a job, except for the very rich, life is made extremely difficult. This is why we go to work. We are not directly coerced into working, but society is structured in

---

19   See also David Graeber, *Bullshit Jobs: a theory* (Penguin, 2018).

such a way that we must work. In the event of a job loss, over a third of households would be unable to pay the coming month's rent.[20] It might, especially in an economic downturn, be difficult to find another job of the same quality, pay or location. The world outside of work is one of punitive benefit sanctions and moral condemnation. The threat of paltry benefits or of losing our homes leaves us vulnerable to worse treatment: we, almost always, need a job more than a job needs us. Our entrance into work is unfree, and while we're there, our time is not our own.

Wanting work

In September 2020, an advert on London's Tube, paid for by the cleaning products company Dettol, caused online controversy after it listed what its authors assumed were positives about working in an office and the manifold joys of commuting.[21]

Hearing an alarm. Putting on a tie. Carrying a handbag. Receptionists. Caffeine-filled air. Taking a lift. Seeing your second family. Watercooler conversations. Proper bants.

Deserved scorn was poured on the advert. Not only were Dettol implicitly supporting a dubiously safe return to workplaces for those who could, by and large, work from home; they were also running against the grain of years of popular culture that depict the office not as an environment in which desires are met but one in which they are frustrated. This is, in some ways, the popular common sense. The office is where you go to do

---

20   https://theguardian.com/money/2016/aug/09/england-one-in-three-families-one-months-pay-losing-homes-shelter-study (last accessed December 2020).

21   https://indy100.com/article/dettol-ad-office-tube-work-benefits-9703071 (last accessed December 2020).

something you don't particularly enjoy, and usually, make small talk with people you aren't particularly interested in. However, despite such widespread griping and groaning about workplace culture, there was something I found troubling in the response to the advert. Many people report actually enjoying work; a 2017 poll found that two thirds of people in the UK claim to like or love their job. Only one in ten said they disliked their job.[22] How do we square this with the sorts of problems a critic of work under capitalism might find in work?

Nothing I've said so far – and nothing I'll argue in this book – excludes the possibility that some people might enjoy their jobs. Clearly, not everybody is unhappy at work. The much-maligned Dettol advert implies not just that work is enjoyable, but that people have strong emotional connections to it: they might even miss it. For many, work is the place in which their lives are lived, in which some of their most important relationships are forged and in which they might find meaning, even joy. It is important that critics of work reckon with this. However, this is not a book about people's subjective preferences so much as the conditions in which those preferences are formed, and the background of possibilities against which they exist, such as the lack of other sources of possible fulfilment and sociability. It is a consideration of the ways in which capitalist work curtails people's freedom, how even while it might provide some satisfaction, even some pleasure, it does so at the expense of the cultivation of other kinds of pleasures, of other ways of living and producing, together. It aims to make sense of the harms of actually existing work and to grapple with the kinds of ways we could make that work better. In the first part of the book, I outline what work is, how it has been understood and contested.

22 https://yougov.co.uk/topics/politics/articles-reports/2017/08/03/love-wage-balance-how-many-brits-their-job-and-the (last accessed December 2020).

INTRODUCTION: WORK'S FANTASY

The second part of the book is concerned with what it is that work does – to society, to us as individuals, and to the areas of lives that are becoming more and more work-like, particularly to leisure and to education. In the final section, I consider what we ought to do about the problem of work.

Work is tied up with our identities and our everyday lives in profound ways. We are encouraged to love our jobs and live the 'values' of the companies we work for. Communities are shaped by and around certain industries (and the decline of those industries). This means that when we criticise work, we often come up against fear and confusion. This fear is not merely the product of a work ethic promulgated by elites. Given that, under capitalism, work becomes the only avenue for self-development, respect and fulfilment, this is a genuine fear of a loss of self. But capitalism's defining feature – work, wage labour – is a curtailment of the possibilities of our lives. We can't get our lives back without radically changing the very foundations of society.

Chapter 1

Work, capitalism and capitalist work

> Those who take their seats on golden chairs to write
> Will be interrogated about those others who
> Wove their robes for them – Bertolt Brecht[1]

After years of hearing the Thatcherite mantra that 'There Is No Alternative', new leftist movements across the globe have shown that there might, after all, be an alternative to austerity and neoliberalism. This puncturing of the ideological status quo has had one particularly odd fallout: since the Great Financial Crisis of 2008, and its attendant political mobilisations, mainstream political commentators have begun to talk about capitalism. In some ways, this is progress. Naming capitalism as a particular system rather than just the ways things are naturally and inevitably, is in one way, better than taking capitalism as a given. But despite this, mainstream attempts to analyse capitalism remain shallow. Capitalism is something, the argument goes, that compels us, or companies, to act in harmful ways, but not something we can do very much about. This argument is typically expressed as something like a shrug. It

---

1   Bertolt Brecht, 'How future ages will judge our writers', trans. Tom Kuhn & David Constantine, in *The collected Poems of Bertolt Brecht*, (New York & London: W. W. Norton, 2018), p. 752.

excuses individual choices – buying some particularly expensive or violently produced commodity, or one that is both, like, say, AirPods – or for corporate exploitation. Its answer to why companies or individual capitalists behave the way that they do is 'Eh, that's capitalism for you!'

As the writer Rachel Connolly puts it, such accounts are 'curiously flat.'[2] They, she argues, mask the vast differences in experience and degrees of capitalist oppression, claiming instead a classless millennial malaise, equivocating between mere participation and active complicity. While there might be an alternative to capitalism or its neoliberal variant plausible in such accounts, it remains under-theorised. This is because the stated 'flatness' extends beyond the ethics of individual or corporate actions to the very understanding of how capitalism works. In this flattened account, things happen in a capitalist way because that's just how capitalism works. In such accounts, our individual actions are irrelevant – which may well be the case, as alone we can't do very much – but crucially, so is collective political action. It's hard to see how beyond the most superficial level, this mechanical account significantly differs from 'There Is No Alternative'.

Even outside of mainstream discourse, among those who know themselves to have a problem with capitalism, there is a trace of the same problem. Capitalism becomes an enclosed, fixed and mechanical system. X, Y or Z happens because of capitalism. This might be true, but it's banal. As those interested in changing the world, seriously changing it, not just curbing its worst effects, we need to actually figure out what capitalism is like. This might seem like a pointless, academic exercise: we already know it's bad! Why do we need to work out exactly what

---

2   https://thebaffler.com/latest/this-brand-is-late-capitalism-connolly (last accessed December 2020).

it is or consider the ways in which it's bad? But without knowing the internal dynamics of capitalism, how it works, and how it affects us, as individuals and at the level of the social whole, we can neither make sense of it nor change it. It's not enough to say that capitalism is bad, we have to explain why and how, and imagine and fight for alternatives.

One way to think about these two 'hows' is through the prism of work. This is a particularly helpful route because the way we work under capitalism is not contingent but rather a fundamental feature of capitalism. It's also something which, for most of us, makes the harder 'how' questions easier to grapple with on an everyday basis. The first step to answering these questions is the subject of this chapter, working out what capitalism is by considering the place of work within it, and the particular, historically specific features of capitalist work. It looks at one particular kind of work: garment production.

A stitch in time; the history of garment manufacturing

When we buy or wear clothes we rarely think about the amount of effort, the hours of people's lives, that went into producing them. Most of us have no idea how cloth is made, how clothes are cut, sewn and finished. We encounter clothes in the same way we do other goods for sale. We see the very end of the production: the design of the shop, the overfamiliar email from a brand, the sponsored content on Instagram. At the other end of the chain, workers, usually in the Global South, work long hours producing textiles and clothing.

Garment production has long been associated with women. Today, the majority of garment workers across the world are women.[3] Most are paid next to nothing – only 2% of garment workers are paid a liveable wage, calculated on local housing and food, education and childcare costs.[4] In Ancient Greece, the birth of a baby girl was marked with a tuft of wool by the door of the family's house.[5] In Homer's *Odyssey* (c. 8th century BCE), Penelope, waiting for the safe return of her husband, tells her would-be suitors that she will not marry until she has finished weaving a burial shroud for Odysseus' father, Laertes. Every night, she undoes the weaving she had done that day. A clever trick, possibly suggestive of the gendered dimensions of weaving, as for it to work, the technical knowledge of weaving has to be a primarily female possession. Similarly, when Sappho writes of the suffering of lovesickness, it is weaving that she is unable to continue: 'sweet mother I cannot work the loom/I am broken with longing for a boy by slender Aphrodite'.[6]

We know that clothes – originally, animal skins and cloth spun from natural fibres, offering protection from extremes of temperature – were invented between 42,000 and 72,000 years ago. We can work this out because of a strange fact: during this period, head lice and body lice diverge as species, adapting to their different environments. For head lice to exist as a separate species, there are probably clothes.[7]

Clothing, and the technologies involved in its production, might have initially developed out of physiological necessity, but became a means for public displays of power, status and

---

3 85% of those employed in the garment industry are women, see https://waronwant.org/sweatshops-bangladesh (last accessed December 2020).

4 https://fashionrevolution.org/usa-blog/how-much-garment-workers-really-make/ (last accessed December 2020).

5 Kassia St Clair, *The Golden Thread* (London: John Murray, 2019), p. 13.

6 Anne Carson, *If Not, Winter: Fragments of Sappho* (New York: Vintage, 2003), p. 203.

7 St Clair, *The Golden Thread*, pp. 25–6.

identity. In early human societies, the production of cloth could be a communal affair, the production itself a social ritual. Some surviving ancient cloth has wefts crossed in the middle, meaning that two people must have been working on it simultaneously.[8]

Necessity, even the most basic physiological kind, is rarely something simple – not even in prehistoric society, as was the case with cloth. Needs are met within a context that deems some ways of meeting them more appropriate or more pleasant than others. Even the meeting of 'simple' needs, then, is more complex than we might assume. Clothing also designates particular social roles – a wedding ring, a ballgown, a business suit – not to mention the functionality of overalls or protective gear. It makes it possible to work out someone's place in society with only the briefest glance and has done so for thousands of years. Historically, certain colours or fabrics were legally designated for certain types of people – yellow for women in Ancient Greece, for example. Legislation against certain classes wearing certain fabrics or colours proliferated, to prevent people posing as belonging to different ranks than their proper ones.

Making cloth, whether, from wool, flax or cotton is time-consuming. Natural fibres are spun into thread, then woven into cloth. The cloth is then sewn into garments. For the vast majority of human history, this process was done by hand, typically by women, and within individual households. Some of this work was done for clothing and furnishing the household itself, and some of it for pay or for trade. From the fifteenth century on, workers in Britain were supplied with materials and worked within their homes to produce cloth for merchants to sell on. In 1750, spinning was the most common form of paid employment

---

8   Elizabeth Wayland Barber, *Women's Work: The First 20,000 Years* (New York & London, W.W. Norton & Company, 1994), pp. 23–4.

for women.[9] By the end of the eighteenth century, cloth-making, moved from homes to factories. Following a series of techno-logical innovations and the availability of cheap, often child labour, the production of cloth was subject to industrialisation, moving to expanding factories. The cloth in question, replacing wool's centuries-long hegemony, was cotton, imported from slave plantations across the American South. By the late 1850s, 80% of cotton imports to Britain were from the US, with raw cotton, picked by slaves, making up 60% of the total value of US exports.[10]

While the production of cloth moved from the home to the factory, sewing and the production of garments tended to take place on a much smaller scale, in workshops and sweatshops rather than in dark satanic mills. Before the nineteenth century, most people made their own clothes or altered second-hand clothes. The wealthy had clothes specially made for them. Two nineteenth-century developments sped up the production of cloth. The first of these is well-known: new machinery, estimated to have increased productivity ten or elevenfold following its introduction in the US.[11] The techniques used to produce garments from fabric today differ very little from those at the turn of the last century. The second and more decisive factor was the development of standard clothes sizes. Perhaps surprisingly, these innovations were made with men in mind, namely sailors, who did not have time to wait for tailored clothes to be made during their brief time on land. The wars of the mid-nineteenth century sped up the development of standard sizes. The need to clothe thousands of men at great speed, particularly for the

---

9   St Clair, *The Golden Thread*, p. 16.

10   Ibid., p. 172.

11   Nancy L. Green, *Ready to Wear and Ready to Work* (Durham & London: Duke University Press, 1997), p. 38.

American Civil War, stimulated demand and reorganised supply. In peacetime, these new, mechanised supply chains were turned to civilian markets.[12] Through new department stores and mail-order catalogues, clothes were marketed and sold in larger and larger numbers to more and more people. While this was not the first time that garments were used to display identity, the massification of this possibility, and that it became a public leisure activity mark a significant change in the history of consumption and of consumerism.

By 1900, a ready-made garment could be made in approximately one third to one half of the time it took to hand sew one. Clothes are produced seasonally – we wear different things in winter than in summer – and are changed in line with new trends. This feature of nature, seasonality, has effects on production, making economies of scale harder as there are two busy periods of garment production a year followed by a slack period. This makes production resistant to deeper mechanisation or automation – the upfront costs of equipment become all the more prohibitive if these machines won't be used for parts of the year. This also keeps the size of the workplaces small, unlike the factories in which fabrics are produced. Brands outsource the production of clothing to suppliers, who themselves often further outsource. At the bottom of the chain are homeworkers who take on additional work in times of high demand or who add decorative detail. Contracts are awarded to buyers based on low prices. With upfront costs low, buyers' profits rely on squeezing as much work from their employees as possible. This, along with the heaviness and heat of the work, is where the term 'sweatshop' comes from.

At first, large-scale garment production took place in the Global North. In cities like London, New York and Paris, migrant

---

12   Ibid., p. 23.

workers toiled long hours for low wages, in small shops, often in the homes of their employers. As New York's garment workers began to organise, manufacturers moved their shops to states with less well-organised workforces and less stringent labour laws. Relocating garment production is very easy: its machinery, materials and end products are light. Later, these supply chains were extended across national borders, as markets opened up for cheap labour. Between 1990 and 2004, the number of workers employed in the textile or clothing manufacturing sector in the US reduced by 60%.[13] Production moved to the Caribbean, to Mexico, to Central America, and then to China and the rest of Asia, particularly to South Asia.

As well as seasonal variation and new seasonal looks – set by fashion houses and filtered down through the high street – brands respond to the accelerating turn-over of trends by designing, producing, and selling clothes more quickly. To do this at the required speed, some outsourced production has even returned to the Global North. The demand for extremely fast fashion, produced in short batches, shipped and delivered in the shortest possible window, worn by an Instagram influencer one day, and arriving through the customer's postbox the very next, has brought garment production back to places like Leicester. Between 2008 and 2016, the turnover of apparel manufacturers in the East Midlands grew by 110%.[14] This allows for short supply chains. It takes only a week for a batch of clothing to be finished, ready for sale. The small clothing runs – about 1,000 units – are frequent but unpredictable. This means that the factories, often

13   Ashok Kumar, *Monopsony Capitalism* (Cambridge, UK: Cambridge University Press, 2020), p. 68.

14   Nikolaus Hammer and Réka Plugor, 'Disconnecting Labour? The Labour Process in the UK Fast Fashion Value Chain', *Work, Employment and Society* 33, no. 6, December 2019, pp. 1–16, 6.

subcontracted, sometimes multiple times, cannot run at full capacity. The pressure to produce clothes more cheaply can only be met by extremely exploitative working conditions, including paying below the minimum wage (the industry norm is around £3 per hour[15]) by faking pay slips to short-change migrant workers. Add to this, the refusal of breaks, lack of employment contracts, and expectations of extreme flexibility, with workers expected to stop and start working in line with orders. Workplaces are often segmented, with different wages and expectations of flexibility for different groups, often tied to immigration status.

At the other end of the value chain, influencers and celebrities are sent clothes to advertise. The amount of collective effort that goes into shaping consumer demand is nearly inconceivable; it takes a lot of work to create the feeling of needs for new clothes. The influencer's post looks effortless and authentic, but it hides the extensive work of producing the emotional and logistical preconditions for the selling of commodities produced elsewhere.

Free and forced work; the dynamics of capitalism

The conditions faced by garment workers from the late nineteenth century up until today are frighteningly similar. Workers' stories of collapses and fires, of sexual harassment, of the physical and emotional toll of demanding work, would immediately make sense to each other across the centuries.

From this brief and provisional history, we can determine some important historical changes. The first of these is a change in how the need for clothing is met. For most of human life, this was met by individual activity, outside of the market – you

15   Ibid., p. 10.

sewed clothes for yourself. Later, this became a paid activity. Under industrial capitalism, however, it does not move into the factory, as cloth-making does. It moves to a smaller shop, while remaining partly in the home.

Crucially, the work of making cloth and later of sewing clothes becomes something done almost entirely by paid workers. While paid work in cloth making and to a lesser extent in garment production predated industrial capitalism, the proportion of cloth and clothes produced within the market, for a wage, and with the goods produced done so for sale to a third party shifted significantly in this period. Rather than goods produced by individual households, they are made in the market, by workers paid a wage. In the case of cloth and garment production, this could be an hourly rate or a piece rate. Those workers use their wages to pay for other goods, other necessities and other luxuries. For this to take place, workers have to be separated from the means of production. Rather than some natural human tendency to exchange, people had to be made into workers through a violent separation, removing them, forcibly, from the means of production. This happens at different speeds and within different extents of violence for different kinds of production. The first dispossession, from the land, is particularly violent. As Marx puts it, this expropriation 'is written in the annals of mankind in letters of blood and fire'.[16]

Released from the old ties of feudalism, the worker is 'free' to enter into a contract with an employer. Workers can sell the use of their particular skills and capacities to any buyer. This is a dubious freedom because it takes place against a background of coercion – if you don't 'freely' contract, you won't be able to survive. In the contemporary UK, the welfare benefits system

16   Karl Marx, *Capital Vol 1* (London: Penguin, 1990), p. 875.

won, at least in part, by workers in the twentieth century, means that you, provided you can navigate the system and are eligible for benefits (itself not a given), can (try to) survive without a job. Restrictions, conditionality and cuts introduced to the benefits system, however, mean there is intense pressure on claimants to return to waged work. The balance of power within this contract can be skewed towards employers, too. Workers could be imprisoned for leaving contracts of employment early, without the permission of their employer, until the mid-1870s.[17]

Capitalism depends on the worker, separated from the means of production who enters contract-bound employment. But capitalism depends on unfree labour just as much as it has on illusory 'free' labour. Capitalist work depends on the continued existence of unfree and forced labour across value chains. For cotton production, this was antebellum chattel slavery in the eighteenth and nineteenth centuries, and today, the exploitation of incarcerated labour, where US prisoners, including at the Louisiana State Penitentiary, where nearly 80% of inmates are Black,[18] pick cotton for a pittance. Work activity that sits outside of the dominant mode of wage labour – slavery, unpaid work and forced work – can function as a precondition for wage labour; the outside that means the inside is possible.

The second change comes from the particular kind of power over workers that employers have under capitalism. While we shouldn't imagine that before capitalism, production was not overseen by those with power, or that there was not particular pressure on workers, say, at particular times of the year, to work in certain ways or at certain speeds. But, a fundamental

17   https://viewpointmag.com/2014/09/02/the-political-economy-of-capitalist-labor/ (last accessed December 2020).

18   https://theatlantic.com/politics/archive/2015/09/a-look-inside-angola-prison/404377/ (last accessed December 2020).

feature of capitalism is what's termed the 'profit motive', the drive, on the part of those who own the means of production, to accumulate capital. As Ellen Meiksins Wood charts in her history of the development of capitalism, the property relations in early modern Britain that established this dispossession that created workers, 'would set in motion a relentless compulsion to compete, to produce cost-effectively, to maximise profit, to reinvest surpluses, and systematically to increase labour productivity by improving the productive forces'.[19] This puts employers in a political (in the sense of pertaining to power) relationship with workers. They want to maximise profits, which can mean squeezing as much as possible out of their employees. This can amount to more or less violent techniques of management, from extending the hours of the working day, stopping employers from taking breaks or docking wages for not meeting particular standards. Or it can mean softer techniques of control that attempt to align the interests of employers and employees, like seniority rules. It also means that when profits are not possible in a particular sector or geographic location, they might abandon it, looking for cheaper labour elsewhere.

This relation and the daily indignities and exploitations it brings at work are a central way through which capitalism as a social formation is lived. But it is lost or ignored in much mainstream discussion of the contemporary garment industry, which tends to focus on the ethics of consumption, whether through buying less or buying better. This – the privileging of a set of questions for consumers over questions of work and labour rights – has a history as old as the garment industry itself. In the 1880s, the New York sweatshops in which migrant garment

19   Ellen Meiksins Wood, *The Origin of Capitalism* (London & New York: Verso, 2017), p. 94.

workers toiled became of growing concern to the middle classes. One response to this now visible social problem was the founding of consumer campaigns. The Consumers' League preached the responsibility of consumers and worried about the healthiness of sweatshop-produced clothing. They proposed special labels for sweatshop-free clothing. Their campaigning anticipated the consumer-based activism of more than a century later.

The problems associated with garment production are broadly grouped under the management imperative of 'flexibility', or the need to squeeze labour costs as far as possible; the importance to profits of the ability to hire and fire at will. These problems cannot be solved by consumer attempts to change patterns of demand. The model of outsourcing allows brands and producers to dodge accountability. As stories of abuse in the garment industry re-emerge, new consumer campaigns in the style of the Consumers' League are popping up. Sometimes these campaigns are little more than a branding exercise by companies themselves. One such company sews a tag into each of its jumpers that allows customers to check in on the progress of the sheep the wool for their jumper has come from. When the supply chain of garments is considered, the rights of animals to be treated well comes above consideration for human workers. The appeal of this sort of thing is not hard to see. Shopping makes people feel guilty about the violence committed for their purchases. Consumers are confronted with the ambiguity of the need to shop, and guilt at their relative privilege. Providing information on how goods are made and removing violence in that chain (as far as possible) can comfort confused consumers.

If consumer campaigns do little to help, what then will work? One strategy has been to involve international bodies through codes and audits. A regime of inspections and minimum standards has done little to change conditions, however.[20] The real impetus for change has come from workers collectively organising, from building worker power. As Ashok Kumar puts it, 'it was workers – not the employers – who have eliminated US factory fires to date'.[21]

Today's shopper has very little idea about how their clothes are made or what they're made of. Our relationship with clothes and fabric has changed dramatically over the course of the last two centuries. We've gone from knowing how to make fabric, how to sew and repair clothes, to not knowing how to sew on a button. Usually this is painted as a story of decline: we don't value the things we have and greedily buy more and more of what we don't need. This might be the case, but it misses out the history of production from the side of the workers. Plus, we shouldn't assume that our consumer needs are natural or fixed any more than capitalism itself is. This doesn't mean we can easily abandon them though, but rather that marketing, social pressure, the expectation that our identity be expressed through consumption (and the evisceration of other avenues for its expression) conspire to make these 'needs' feel urgent and deep. The creation of new needs is part of capitalism's hunger for growth, creating more and more commodities and felt-needs, expanding across more and more of the globe.

History and myths

The garment industry shows us how the conditions of work change – from within a household to outside of it. It's not that pre-industrial life was idyllic, peaceful, or non-exploitative. That

---

20 https://aflcio.org/sites/default/files/2017-03/CSReport.pdf (last accessed December 2020).

21 Kumar, *Monopsony Capitalism*, p. 45.

most people no longer know how to make fabric or sew clothes is not something bad, except perhaps insofar as it makes people more reliant on the market. New technologies and labour-saving processes can be good things: the problem is who owns the technology required for these processes and in whose interest that technology is developed and run. At the moment, the infra-structure of production is geared towards maximising profit. The terms on which workers are hired and what they do in their role is decided by management. In unionised industries, trade unions can negotiate what these terms are, but rarely do workers get to decide for themselves what they do. The quality, variety and even just number of tasks available to any given worker are often out of their control, too. As much as qualifications and skill are important in finding work, so is luck, particularly whether you're born at a time of plentiful jobs, or at a time, like now, when the spectres of job losses and the growing dominance of the gig economy loom large. These are particular threats for young people, 60% of those who lost their job between June and August 2020, in the Covid-19 pandemic, were between 18 and 24.[22]

From the present, capitalism can look inevitable, albeit crisis-ridden, as if a chain reaction of vast impersonal forces simply submerged us all. It is in this smooth, ahistorical way that the story of work is often told. In one variant of the story – proposed by the economist Adam Smith – people have a natural 'propensity to truck, barter, and exchange', and this natural propensity leads nicely to the division of labour and modern capitalism. This origin myth is taken to task by Marx in *Capital*. Rather than some natural human tendency to exchange, people had to be made into workers: the conditions for capitalism –

22   https://www.theguardian.com/business/2020/oct/13/uk-redundancies-rise-covid-unemployment-rate-furlough-scheme (last accessed December 2020).

accumulation and the existence of 'free' wage labourers – come from human action.

In another origin story, human genius unleashes Promethean technological forces; a series of inventions change society forever. In this version, we are presented with a continuous jump from the ancient production of linen to contemporary technology that allows you to point your phone at someone's shirt and buy the same one. Instead of by real living humans, the jump is powered by technology. Technology – in this case, taken to mean individual inventions of singular, historically top-hatted (now Steve Jobs turtleneck-ed) – unleashes new forces, changing social relations, making more and bigger profits. The actual lives of ordinary people are hidden in this story. Factories pop up, as if dropped from above by gods rather than built by real people, canals raise themselves up from the earth, crops tend to themselves.

Microsoft founder, Bill Gates, coined the term 'friction-free capitalism' to describe a future of maximally efficient markets, with the internet sweeping away traditional market imperfections like physical distance and varying local regulation. Whether this easy movement is projected backwards or forwards, it obscures the real friction of the real world. A lot of this friction comes from human action, shaped by the mobilisation of groups and individuals, by ideas, or merely by chance or contingency. Sometimes technology doesn't work smoothly or improve exponentially, and how it is used is shaped by politics in real societies and particularly in real workplaces. Sometimes technology is unable to mechanise or automate a task because it is complex in a particular way or requires a degree of dexterity not yet possible.

Plus, technology can be expensive to buy and to maintain. Consider the decline of the mechanical car washes that used to be found on most petrol station forecourts in the 1990s. These machines, first developed in the 1970s, have had their position on petrol station forecourts usurped. They have been replaced not by the dazzling new robotic technologies of Boston Dynamics, but by manual car-washing.[23] Machines are expensive to buy and maintain, and in the place of mechanical car washes have sprung up thousands of small, hand car wash firms, many of which are unlicensed and with plenty of evidence of extreme exploitation of migrant workers. They often straddle the formal and informal sectors. Car washes are one of the most commonly reported sites of labour exploitation according to the Modern Slavery Helpline run by the NGO Unseen.[24] How we work is shaped not by technology alone, but by existing relations of power. When labour does not have much power, particularly in the context of low wages, there is little pressure to automate jobs.

Against this Promethean account of technology or Smith's imaginary barterer, we can trace a history of capitalism and capitalist work as human action. What's important in this account is the uniqueness of capitalism as a way of organising society: it is one in which human needs are met and forged in the market. It presupposes the separation of the methods of producing from those who produce. This separation creates and sustains a power relation that shapes or conditions the rest of social life. These conditioning dynamics of ownership sustain capitalism. But capitalism is also shaped by contingencies of nature, like the fact that seasonality means a low season for garment production, or that irregularities in wood's texture

23   https://theguardian.com/commentisfree/2016/dec/12/mark-carney-britains-car-wash-economy-low-wage-jobs (last accessed December 2020).

24   https://publications.parliament.uk/pa/cm201719/cmselect/cmenvaud/981/981.pdf (last accessed December 2020).

and grain combined with the detail required for domestic furniture meant that hand production, rather than industrial or even mechanised production of furniture, remained common throughout the nineteenth century.[25]

While the violence of primitive accumulation, of this early dispossession, might have receded, it has not gone away. Despite the centrality of 'free' contract-bound work to capitalism, there are more people in slavery today than at any other point in history. And the majority of the world's population (60%) work in the informal or shadow sector, outside of contract-bound employment.[26] Direct and indirect violence is found in the formal sector too, although typically to a lesser extent. The American historian and writer, Studs Terkel, gathered accounts of ordinary American's working lives for his 1974 book *Working*. He began his book by writing that '[t]his book, being about work, is, by its very nature, about violence.'[27] The same holds for the book you're holding in your hands now.

Rather than accept the circular logic of the mock critique of capitalism offered by mainstream political commentators – one that says that things are capitalist and bad because they're capitalist but there's not much we can do – this book hopes to make sense of the violence that might be said to characterise capitalist work; and to put that violence in the context of political relationships, of human agency and of human action. In short, how and in which sorts of ways things could be different.

25   Alexandra Armstrong, 'The Wooden Brain: Organizing Untimeliness in Marx's *Capital*' *Mediations* 31.1, Fall 2017, pp. 3–26, 7.).

26   https://ilo.org/global/about-the-ilo/newsroom/news/WCMS_627189/lang--en/index.htm (last accessed December 2020).

27   Studs Terkel, *Working* (New York: Ballantine Books, 1974) p. XIII.

Chapter 2

Contesting 'work'

The capital given in exchange for labour-power is converted into necessaries, by the consumption of which the muscles, nerves, bones, and brains of existing labourers are reproduced, and new labourers are begotten.[1] – Karl Marx

Homelessness is an acceptable humiliation. Drudgery is another. But selling sex on the other hand is everyone's business.[2] – Virgine Despentes

Capitalism's dispossessed worker is 'free' to sell their labour power, but what are the sources of their labour power: what sustains their ability to work? How are their physical and physiological needs, the ones that mean they can get up and go back to work again tomorrow, and the ones that sustain the existence of a class of propertyless workers across time, met? One way is through the wage and the market; renting or buying a home, buying food, paying for particular services. But some of these needs are not met in the market, obtained through wages, or are only partly, or sometimes, met that way. In some cases, it might be the state that reproduces their labour power and readies them to work another day. This state-coordinated activity might be more

---

1   Marx, *Capital*, p. 717.
2   Virgine Despentes, *King Kong Theory* (London: Fitzcarraldo, 2020), p. 55.

or less coercive and violent; we might think of the education system, the healthcare system, the welfare and benefits system. The state tends to be interested in two cases: the reproduction of workers over the longer term, as in the scale of the lifetime, and stepping in to prevent the most serious harms when the wage and market are insufficient to cover reproductive needs. There is also another activity, one which has been naturalised, made to look like it's nothing to do with capitalism, and merely a refuge from it rather than an important constituent part of it. This is the unwaged work done within the home, typically by women. This third kind of activity – housework – has been the subject of feminist debates and a source of feminist organising. Through feminism's theoretical and practical mobilisations, the category or concept of 'work' itself was called into question.

Before looking at that particular history and other challenges to what 'work' is, it's worth dedicating some time to disentangling semantic threads. 'Work' is used to describe all manner of activities. Some of these seem to have little in common beyond requiring *effort*: we might work on ourselves, work in a particular location, sometimes for pay or sometimes with a modifier like 'voluntary' in front of it and some people are just *hard work*. Britney Spears' 2013 'Work Bitch' manages to capture most of the typical applications of 'work': working (i.e., expending physical effort to improve) for a 'hot body', and working (i.e., making money through paid work) for 'a Bugatti', 'a Maserati', 'a Lamborghini', and 'a big mansion'. The equivocation between the two kinds of work allows the song to bring to the fore a third possible kind of 'work', the expending of a sexualised embodied effort, urging listeners to 'work it hard like it's your profession'. This is a particular working of the body, of making it appealing, of dancing – it's a song after all. Amid Britney's broad invocation of 'work' as effort of various kinds, the narrower definition of work rears its head.

'Work' can be immensely general, near enough to a generic form of expending effort, it is also particular, typically being used to mean paid work, a place of work, a job. This means that the same activity can be both work and not-work depending on the conditions in which it is undertaken. So, scrubbing floors in someone else's home is work when done for pay, but not work, at least in the narrow sense, when done to keep your own home clean. Similarly, uploading a picture to Instagram, writing the caption, engaging with any comments, and so on, are not work when done on your own time, but *are* work when your job is managing the social media accounts of a company, or perhaps when you're an influencer, posting sponsored content on behalf of a brand. The same holds for playing video games, which can be a purely leisure activity or a form of work in the narrow sense. While leisure and work are often opposed to each other, some argue that the once-discreet activities bleed into each other under contemporary capitalism, a topic that will be explored in Chapter 6.

There are two concepts related to that of work – labour and toil. Both denote particularly hard work, especially physical work, *laborious* work. Labour has another meaning, too, that of workers in general. Unlike labour and toil, work isn't necessarily exhausting – it's neutral on the extent of effort required, although it does always require *some* effort. Even the broadest account of 'work' wouldn't allow someone who was only sitting down or otherwise resting to be working, unless for some very specific purpose.

But the subject of this enquiry is not effort in general, or work in general, but work under capitalism. What is important to note about the semantic slipperiness of work is that the generic or broad use of 'work' as expending effort and the narrow use of 'work' as meaning paid expending of effort tracks a cleavage between paid activity and the often unpaid reproductive activity that is a precondition of that paid activity.

The hidden abode's hidden abode

Karl Marx is most famous as a critic of capitalism, but at the heart of his critique can be found a desperate plea for the transformation of work. People, he argues, express themselves and create the world through creative and collective activity. This natural tendency is twisted into something unrecognisable in work under capitalism. He didn't just think work around him was bad because it took place in noisy and dangerous conditions, or for low wages and long hours. The problem of work was a fundamental one: under capitalism, work takes something human and turns it into something monstrous. The forces of capital become ravenous, eating up all that is human, sucking on the very lifeblood of society. Marx's account is compelling; our jobs do leave us feeling chewed up, spit out, and too tired for anything other than the meeting of the most basic needs.

To make his case, Marx argues against the fairy tales of mainstream economic history, in which a natural human propensity to exchange bubbles gently into the modern division of labour.[3] This mythical history removes the violence of the early stages of capitalism and of industrial capitalism. Against this, Marx presents to us the 'hidden abode' of capitalism, looking beyond exchange to production.[4] Recall that, on Marx's account, the worker exchanges labour power, in a dubiously 'free' exchange, for wages. But what are the sources of labour power? How is

---

3   Marx, *Capital*, Chapter 26, p. 873.
4   Ibid., p. 279.

labour power itself produced? To answer this question, we need to turn away from Marx and towards feminist theorists who have looked into the hidden abode's own hidden abode.

To reproduce labour power, to make it possible for the worker to return to work the following day, requires the meeting of a minimal set of physical and psychological needs (food, shelter and comfort). Some of these can be met within the market, say, paying rent, buying prepared food, paid for with wages. But, as feminists have argued, this is only part of the picture. Rather than being met in the market, a great deal of social reproduction is done by women for free, in the home. Exactly what the balance of market and non-market social reproduction is will depend on what the society in which it takes place is like, on differences in family and household structures, in the role of the state, as well as what the socially determined needs, those above the most minimal ones are.

The feminist social reproduction contention is that by not paying sustained attention to the dynamics of social reproduction, in particular, to unpaid work in the home, a potentially significant terrain of exploitation and political struggle is obscured from view. There are significant disagreements on whether the exploitation of unpaid household work produces profit and on the extent to which the social role of the housewife determines women's overall societal standing, but there is agreement among social reproduction theorists that anti-capitalists need to reckon – theoretically and practically – with this particular area of unpaid work.

The housework debates

In the mid-twentieth century, women's resentment about housework exploded into public consciousness. This work was work they, almost exclusively, did and did with little recognition. Housework is isolating – you're alone in your home all day – and its particular temporality – wiping things that will only become dirty again in a few hours – can be especially deadening. This individualised suffering was made public, but the solutions offered to the problem of housework (the unfair and gendered distribution of tedium) by various feminist traditions differed significantly. The liberal feminist tradition stressed the harms done to individual women by their exclusion from the main workforce and the psychologically stunting effects of the life of the suburban wife. A typical solution was improving women's access to the workforce or other possible sites of recognition outside of the home. Usually, this was through a combination of market solutions to reduce the time individual women spent on housework and childcare, like hiring nannies or cleaners, and efforts to remove barriers of entry to work, including the better public provision of childcare, combatting stereotypes and providing education and training to women. In some instances, it encouraged men to take up a fairer share of domestic work. This approach tended to focus on the mobility of women as individuals, their ability to enter the paid workforce. It tended to take for granted the possibility that paid work would allow for fulfilment.

A second response to the problem of housework can be found in efforts – theoretical and practical – to communalise it. This approach saw housework as particularly pernicious because it was isolated and needlessly duplicated, with each household doing their own washing, their own cooking, and so on. Community creches, feminist communes and communal cooking reduced the load for each woman and brought her into potentially political contact with her peers. One of the first four demands of the British Women's Liberation Movement, made at the movement's first conference in Oxford in 1970, was free 24-hour creches.[5] Some of these communalising practices were grassroots and anti-state in their political orientation, in such cases, although they might demand public funding, control over their running was intended to remain in the hands of the community. Angela Davis argued similarly that a fair distribution of housework within households did not adequately address the problem of housework, but rather than local communalisations, she makes the case for industrialised and socialised housework. In 'The Approaching Obsolescence of Housework', the final chapter of her 1981, *Women Race and Class,* Davis writes that '[a] substantial portion of the housewife's domestic tasks can actually be incorporated into the industrial economy'.[6] She argues that such a transformation – making housework the responsibility of society at large rather than the burden of individual women – could only be made possible by state subsidisation to ensure that working-class families could benefit, and to make the scaling-up of unproductive work financially viable.[7]

The third feminist solution to the problem of housework is the one that generated and continues to generate the most debate. The first – improving individual women's lot – has been partially achieved, although men still tend to spend fewer hours on housework than women do, and the second – socialising housework – has been largely forgotten, for reasons which will be discussed more fully in Chapter 9. This third proposal overlaps with the second in that its adherents often supported initiatives

---

5   https://bl.uk/sisterhood/articles/womens-liberation-a-national-movement   (last accessed December 2020). The other three initial demands (equal pay; equal educational and job opportunities; free contraception and abortion on demand) have all been met or partially met.

6   Angela Y. Davis, *Women, Race & Class* (London: Penguin Classics, 2019), p. 201.

7   Ibid., p. 209.

that would communalise or partly communalise housework. But they advanced a specific demand in addition to this: that women be paid for the work they do in the home. They contended that women's work in the home produces value and therefore ought to be recognised.

Beginning in Italy in 1972 but rapidly spreading to the UK, the US, Canada and Germany women demanded 'wages for housework'. This was a rather unusual method of making a political demand in that the specifics of the demand – the wage – was of less importance than the effects that making the demand were intended to have.[8] Foremost among these was the claiming of housework as *work*. This meant it was exploitative in the way that waged work was (as well as having additional harms of its own) and that housewives were themselves members of the working class, that their struggle was not merely promoting some sectional interest but part of working-class struggle. It was made against the chauvinism of a male-dominated left that paid little attention to women.

Just as Marx called into question the naturalness of work under capitalism – showing it not as a natural attribute of humanity but a historically specific and violent arrangement – women associated with the Wages for Housework movement sought to show that the unpaid work women did in the home was not out of a natural feminine benevolence, but exploitation secured through direct and indirect coercion. As Silvia Federici put it in 1975: 'Not only has housework been imposed on women, but it has been transformed into a natural attribute of our female physique and personality, an internal need, an aspiration, supposedly coming from the depth of our female character.'[9]

---

8   For a discussion of this see Katrina Forrester, 'Feminist Demands and the Problem of Housework', forthcoming.

9   Silvia Federici, *Revolution at Point Zero* (Oakland: PM Press, 2012), p. 16.

The project of feminism is, in part, a method of calling into question 'the natural'. It problematises what is taken for granted as 'just how things are' or 'just how people naturally are'. This approach was brought to bear on housework by pointing out the years of training and coercion that go into making young girls good at housework. If we are not born but made women, then we are not born but made housewives.

Claiming housework as *work* was intended to open up a horizon of political possibility by denaturalising it and bringing it into political struggle. For such a transformation to take place, a particular account of work – a particular definition of 'work' – needs to be shared by those making the demand and those hearing it. Without the account of work as harmful and something to be refused, present in the campaign's original context, claiming something as 'work' can mean little more than demanding recognition or compensation rather than seeking something more transformative. When something is described as 'work', a set of claims are made not just about that activity but about 'work' too. When we demand that something is understood and treated as work, we are also defining what work is. In the case of Wages for Housework, this claim makes housework exploitative as work is taken to be, and it makes housewives workers, which is to say, important political agents. It contests 'work' and it contests 'class' at the same time.

The history of feminist theory and feminism as a movement is knotty. It's possible to unravel all kinds of different strands without getting close to a clear view of the whole of the movement. Any historical reconstruction is likely to be partial, obscuring some strands as it brings others into view. It's not my contention that this history is the only origin of feminist thinking about the household, merely that it's one that is particularly helpful for showing how the feminist project of denaturalising was brought to bear on the family and housework. As Angela Davis, among others, argued, the Wages for Housework perspective was not always capable of making sense of the racialised experiences of Black women in the Global North, and tended to universalise the household arrangements of a few countries in the Global North though household arrangements differed significantly around the world. In light of this, some Wages for Housework theorists, including Federici, have revised their positions to better accommodate for Black women's experience of denial of family and domestic life. Federici explains this reassessment as a move from '"refusal" to "valorisation" of housework'.[10]

A reassessment of Wages for Housework in light of the significant changes in women's lives and in the economy since the 1970s is also in order. Household roles are, on the whole, much less rigid than they were. If housework is work, it is work done under rather different conditions. There is also a sense in which, albeit partially and conditionally, women are (inadequately) compensated via certain benefits for elements of housework. The housewife and kitchen are the traditional agent and site of social reproduction, respectively. But in contemporary society, social reproduction is just as likely to take place in cheap fast-food restaurants, through takeaways, tied to elongated affective supply chains – working-class migrant women leaving their home countries to work in the Global North, leaving even poorer women to look after their own children. The destruction of social democratic institutions – the extraction of profit from more and more areas of human social life – alongside stagnating wages and longer hours, means social reproduction has been dislodged from the home. From McDonald's to platform apps for nannies, social reproduction has moved out of the private home

---

10   Federici, *Revolution at Point Zero*, p. 1.

but remains privatised, run for profit, often with some of the most exploitative work practices. This kind of shift is paradigmatic of the changes to working conditions and capitalism itself in the last four decades. These changes have seen an intense strain on the household, particularly its women members, which has been left to plug the gap of a receding welfare state.

The fight for legal recognition

Changing the idea of work, of challenging what counts as 'work', is also a question of the law. The state recognises some activity as work whereas other activities are not recognised as work, even if they're paid. Work is, in the eyes of the law, a specific legally bounded entity with rights and responsibilities – on the part of the employer and the employee or worker.[11] These are not contracts made between equals but by two parties with extremely different amounts and types of power. However, they do offer protection to workers, including the right to a written statement of employment particulars, an itemised payslip, the minimum wage, to maternity leave, to reasonable time off and to sick pay. While these rights are fragile and are sometimes ignored by employers even if they'd be held up at tribunal, they are much better than having no possibility of legal recourse. As such, many current labour campaigns are focused on fighting for the legal recognition of certain activities as work. Foremost among these is organising by sex workers which seeks to secure safety, including through their legal rights as workers by the decriminalisation of sex work.

---

11 British law makes a distinction between employees and workers, both of which are employed by firms but to which firms have differing legal responsibilities. See Employment Rights Act 1996: https://legislation.gov.uk/ukpga/1996/18/part/XIV/chapter/III (last accessed December 2020).

Sometimes, arguments for seeing sex work as work rely on accounts of what work is, often flagging the skill, especially emotional skill it involves. When sex worker exclusionary feminists argue that sex work should not be considered as work because that would mean downplaying the violence against women that they claim it instantiates,[12] this also hails a particular account of 'work'; specifically, one in which violence and coercion do not occur. Arguing these approaches which rely on a moral vocabulary of work, Juno Mac and Molly Smith make the case for seeing sex work as work on strategic political grounds, as the best way to secure safety for sex workers and to afford them space to organise.[13] As with the Wages for Housework perspective, Mac and Smith bring sex workers' mobilisations into the history and future of working-class struggles; from sex workers in Ethiopia joining the Confederation of Ethiopian Labour Unions and taking part in a strike that brought down the government in 1974, to occupations of churches in France and the UK, and up to today's struggles for legal recognition from the state and to political recognition from the labour movement.[14] By moving the terms of the debate away from the liberal terrain of choice and empowerment, they radicalise the *work* part of the concept of sex work.[15]

Foster carers have also recently sought both political and legal recognition as workers, and with some success. The IWGB union's branch of foster carers won a landmark victory at an employment appeal tribunal in August 2020. The tribunal

---

12 Andrea Dworkin, 'Prostitution and Male Supremacy', *Michigan Journal of Gender and Law*, Volume 1, Issue 1, 1993, pp. 1–12.
13 Juno Mac & Molly Smith, *Revolting Prostitutes* (London & New York: Verso), pp. 3–4.
14 Ibid., p. 7.
15 Ibid., p. 218.

found that foster carers were council employees and entitled to employment rights. This strengthens their ability to fight for the minimum wage, sick pay, and protection for whistleblowing.[16]

Elsewhere, trade unions have argued, sometimes persuasively, for the legal recognition of activity as employment, rather than self-employment. In 2016, for example, a tribunal found that Uber drivers, represented by the GMB union, were not self-employed and should be entitled to workers' rights including a guaranteed minimum wage and paid holiday leave.[17] This ruling potentially makes it harder for companies, particularly those who operate in the gig economy, to save costs by ducking their responsibilities to the 5 million or so people who work within it. Uber appealed the ruling, but it was upheld at the Court of Appeal. In February 2021, the Supreme Court confirmed that drivers, contra Uber's arguments, are workers.[18] In October 2020, the company spent $200m to overturn a similar law in California, the largest amount spent on any ballot campaign in US history.[19]

That Uber and other employers are willing to spend quite so much money on making sure activity is not legally defined as work shows the lengths companies are prepared to go to avoid paying for the minimum support the law would oblige them to. Similar contentment to squeeze labour and reduce costs to the company can be seen in the practice, typical in the care sector, of not paying care workers for the time it takes them to travel

16   https://iwgb.org.uk/post/landmark-legal-victory-opens-door-to-worker-rights-for-uk-foster-carers (last accessed December 2020).

17   https://theguardian.com/technology/2016/oct/28/uber-uk-tribunal-self-employed-status (last accessed December 2020); https://supremecourt.uk/cases/uksc-2019-0029.html (last accessed December 2020).

18   https://www.bbc.co.uk/news/business-56123668 (last accessed March 2021).

19   https://theguardian.com/commentisfree/2020/nov/12/uber-prop-22-law-drivers-ab5-gig-workers (last accessed December 2020).

between workplaces. In the summer of 2020, another landmark ruling found that the time home care workers – the majority of whom were Black or minority ethnic women and were employed on zero-hours contracts – were entitled to pay for the travelling and waiting time between appointments. They'd previously been paid effectively less than half the minimum wage.[20]

Struggles over definitions of 'work' are not merely the subject of dry academic debate. They determine the legal rights someone has when mistreated. When they're a struggle over political direction they can determine where the attention – practical and theoretical – of the left might be directed. In the case of work associated with women, misrecognition is common, due to its 'naturalness', its taken-for-grantedness and the lack of value placed on it.

Work's conceptual creep

Since the Wages for Housework movement expanded the terrain of 'work', many other activities that would not typically be considered work have been described as such.[21] These acts of re-labelling are often inspired by the work of sociologist Arlie Hochschild. Hochschild's 1983 *The Managed Heart* described how certain jobs involve the management of a worker's own internal emotional states. Air hostesses, for example, are expected to present a particular kind of demeanour regardless of whether their parent has just died or whether the plane is about to crash. This, as you can imagine, takes an emotional toll. The idea of this kind of effort – 'emotional labour' – has

20   https://unison.org.uk/news/2020/09/government-urged-act-major-minimum-wage-win-homecare-workers-says-unison/ (last accessed December 2020).
21   The political theorist and intellectual historian, Katrina Forrester has described this process as 'work creep'.

been applied to all kinds of activity, both waged and non-waged. Gemma Hartley, an American journalist, describes the mental toll of women remembering birthdays and shopping lists as 'emotional labour', for example. Elsewhere, explaining political ideas, tweeting, and supporting one's friends or partner has been described as 'emotional labour'.

When these claims to 'work' are made, it's hard to know exactly what is being suggested. In some cases, the demand seems to be for compensation. In others, it's the acknowledgement and redistribution of an unfair and gendered distribution of effort. Generally, the underlying intention seems to be showing that a given activity requires effort in cases where that effort is hidden. The effects of making obvious something that has been naturalised and invisibilised can be powerful and helpful in making arguments about social justice, but I'm not convinced that it's always helpful to talk about these activities in terms of 'work', at least not without some further clarifications, because the confusion about what exactly claims to 'work' should result in causes all kinds of difficulties. Hochschild, too, has pushed back against the expansion of the idea of 'emotional labour'.[22]

This doesn't mean the paradigm of work has nothing to add in such cases. But it does seem like there is a distinct activity – work – through which capitalists, as a class, profit from the efforts of workers as a class. One important part of this activity is that the employers will always attempt to maximise their profits, which means they have a particular political relationship with their employees: one of control, of power over, and of surveillance and performance management. While unpaid socially reproductive work in the home shares some features with waged work, this direct relation of power is not present.

22 https://theatlantic.com/family/archive/2018/11/arlie-hochschild-housework-isnt-emotional-labor/576637/ (last accessed December 2020).

Social reproduction theory allows us to see how different kinds of societies and different regimes of capitalist exploitation reproduce themselves. It and other contestations of the nature and status of 'work' represent important critical additions to Marx's account of work. It is easy to assume that finding something that looks like a gap in Marx's theory means he has somehow been disproved; that in failing to account for XYZ, he is no longer relevant. This is the kind of thing that right-wing critics enjoy doing. A big 'well actually' on every page or, more politely, hidden into a footnote. The reality is that no theory is static or should be allowed to remain so. To say that there is something not present doesn't mean the whole idea comes tumbling down. What we inherit from past thinkers are critical frameworks, ways of diagnosing societal ills, and attempts to cure them – both theoretically and practically.

Chapter 3

The paradox of new work

A particular style of work looms large in the history and representation of work and particularly of the working class. This is the kind of traditional, stable, production-based jobs, often jobs for life, that were common in parts of the Global North in the middle decades of the last century. We imagine men in blue boiler suits on production lines, moving like machines, united in their boredom. This kind of work, and the societies shaped around it, are often called 'Fordist', after practices pioneered in Henry Ford's car production plants. Fordism wasn't a revolution in technology alone – the production line isn't just a piece of neutral infrastructure. It's also a technology of control. Ford's principle was 'that the man [i.e., the production line worker] . . . must have every second necessary [to do the work] but not a single unnecessary second'.[1]

Each movement of the worker was mapped and measured; the bodies of the workers were as controlled as the machinery they operated. The speed of the production line was set from above, with workers slowing down or speeding up as and when the line dictates. In the late 1960s, historian Ronald Fraser collated personal accounts of workers in all sectors of the economy, from

---

1   Quoted in Huw Benyon, *Working for Ford* (Wakefield: EP Publishing Ltd., 1975), p. 18.

housewives to MPs, factory workers to bricklayers, and even a priest. The dominant emotional landscape of those involved in production is boredom. The following testimonies are typical:

My work comes to me in a completely automatic way, in the gestures of an automaton. [. . .] But underneath this my mind never stops working. It lives by itself. Some call it dreaming, and if so, I am dreaming all day long, five days a week. [. . .] The whole bench dreams like this. It is a gallery of automatons locked in dreams.[2]

A worker in a cigarette factory writes,

[t]ime is what the factory worker sells: not labour, not skill, but time, dreary time. Desolate factory time that passes so slowly compared with the fleeting seconds of the weekend. Monday morning starts with a sigh and the rest of the working week is spent longing for Friday night. Everybody seems to be wishing his life away. And away it goes – sold to the man in the bowler hat.[3]

The term Fordist is used as a metonym for a particular time in history as well as a particular kind of mass factory work, dominated by the production line. The term gained popularity after its early use by the Italian Marxist Antonio Gramsci in the 1930s, but is most typically applied to the decades of prosperity with mass, standardised production between the end of the Second World War and the early 1970s. It's typically bookended on one side by Taylorism – the project of scientific

2   'On the Line', Ronald Fraser (ed), *Work: Twenty Personal Accounts* (Harmondsworth: Pelican: 1968), pp. 97–8.
3   Ibid., p. 12.

workplace management that measured a worker's movements. Taylorism excited Lenin, America's factory-owners and wealthy, suburban housewives alike. On its other side is Toyotism, lean or 'just-in-time' production, that seeks to eliminate waste (of time, of resources, of inventory) on the line and throughout the production process. None of these historical moments should be viewed as total systems but rather as dominant moods or tendencies.

Fordism involved a wager for workers. In exchange for eight hours of boredom at work five days a week were the freer weekends – people worked to live – and a sharp divide between work and leisure. Of course, this type of work, while perhaps a culturally dominant pattern of employment, was not a reality for many people. Women were still excluded from the workplace, not to mention the exploitation of expropriative and extractive processes enacted on Britain's imperial subjects.

In Ronald Fraser's collection, a housewife speaks of the boredom inherent in the kind of work she does:

It is constantly niggling not only to be doing jobs that require so little valuable effort, but also jobs which are mainly concerned with simply keeping level with natural processes – cleaning jobs, whether of objects or for people, which once done are not done for good, and will have to be done all over again, just as if I have not already made the effort the next day, or even within a few hours. There is something so negative about this role that society heaps on to the shoulders of women, that of making sure things do not get dirty, and people do not get unhealthy.[4]

---

4   Ibid., p. 150.

'New work'

The boredom of the Fordist decades, a standard against which we judge other forms of work, encountered a fierce enemy in the promise of new kinds of work in the 1980s. If Fordist work was routine, hierarchical, mind-deadening, mechanical, and tied people to one task, sometimes even one movement, for the rest of their lives, the 'new work' promised itself to be flexible, exciting, fast-paced, based on team-work, and full of variety. Sociologist Richard Sennett described the work ethic of the 'new work': 'it celebrates sensitivity to others; it requires such 'soft skills' as being a good listener and being cooperative; most of all, teamwork emphasises team adaptability to circumstances.' Despite (or perhaps because of) this seemingly attractive flexibility, 'new work' lacked a certain depth: 'For all the psychological heavy breathing which modern management does about office and factory teamwork, it is an ethos of work which remains on the surface of experience. Teamwork is the group practice of demeaning superficiality.'[5] Today's work promises the experience of togetherness, of being part of a collective, but typically delivers something much more competitive and individualistic.

These kinds of changes are often thought through the conceptual lens of 'neoliberalism'. It's worth describing what we might mean when we talk about neoliberalism, as the term – and imprecise uses of it – are all too quickly maligned. By neoliberalism, I mean a conscious, political project, undertaken to break the power of organised labour and develop new methods to extract profit from more and more of human social life, including from the legacy institutions of the welfare state. David

---

5 Richard Sennett, *The Corrosion of Character* (New York & London: Norton, 1999), p. 99.

Harvey describes it as the 'gutting' or 'hollowing out' of social programmes or social institutions.[6] In its promise of breaking through the boredom of mid-twentieth century Fordism, it turns freedom in on itself. In promising freedom, it produces more coercion. As the philosopher, Byung-Chul Han puts it:

> Neoliberalism represents a highly efficient, indeed an intelligent, system for exploiting freedom. Everything that belongs to practices and expressive forms of liberty – emotion, play and communication – comes to be exploited. It is inefficient to exploit people against their will. Allo-exploitation [exploitation carried out by other people] yields scant returns. Only when freedom is exploited are returns maximised.[7]

At the level of the individual, this means the exploitation of what Han (after Johan Huizinga) terms 'homo ludens' – the playful elements of human personality – and the gamification of work. This means the merging of work and leisure, with work increasingly resembling play, and leisure treated as something we can and should make profitable; each hobby a potential 'side gig'.

When you tell people that you're writing a book about work, about what might be wrong with it, and how we might change it, most people start telling you about their jobs. One thing I found particularly fascinating was the seepage between work and play. One friend would send me pictures of the most egregious of these seepages: 'meditation in the product cave'; Trello, a productivity app, reminding its users that 'self-care is the secret

---

6   See David Harvey, *A Brief History of Neoliberalism* (Oxford: Oxford University Press, 2005), especially pp. 2–3, 87–90, 91–3.

7   Byung-Chul Han, *Psycho-Politics* (London and New York: Verso, 2019), p. 3.

for powerful productivity';[8] a Nintendo Switch area in the office; drinks at the end of the workday to celebrate the CEO's birthday; free breakfasts and midday meditation sessions.

While the ludic coworking-space-dwelling start-up-worker might be in some ways paradigmatic of the contemporary economy, they also represent the select few for whom a 'fun job' is possible. This is because the contemporary world of work is increasingly polarised. This polarisation is the fallout from decades of economic stagnation and the neoliberal economic policy pursued by successive governments in the UK, which have resulted in the dramatic growth of the service sector. The number of jobs which are fulfilling or secure is dwindling, particularly in the wake of the 2008 recession. Many workers in the contemporary economy are precarious service workers, cleaning the homes and offices of those with stable jobs, making other people's lives seamless. Then there are those forced into unpaid work, particularly care work, by the cutting back of the welfare state, often caring for sick, elderly, or young relatives around precarious gig work. However, even though those at the bottom aren't offered the perks of 'fun' co-working spaces, they are often expected to enjoy their work and to see their employers as their friends or families. Work is supposed to be fun, even when there's very little that's actually fun about it. The overfamiliar and friendly emails sent from management and the app interfaces and training programmes workers are expected to undertake (often unpaid) presume and encourage enjoyment.

New work – supposedly unleashed from the boredom of Fordism – is flexible, based around the management of emotions (both the worker's emotions and the emotions of customers), undertaken by allegedly decentralised 'teams' over supply chains

---

8   https://blog.trello.com/self-care-for-productivity (last accessed December 2020).

that extend across the global market. Work has the appearance of informality; it is bound up with social relations and personal social capital, promising to be indistinct from sociability – offering friendship, or even family – in both good and bad jobs.

One way to understand what this 'new work' is like is through the figure of the temp. A temp is a temporary worker. Temps are hired through agencies, starting with office temps in 1950s America, and really taking off the following decade.[9] She – and temps are most often women[10] – is hired on a short-term basis. She is already trained and selected for the specific skills a given temporary job requires. They predate neoliberalism's dominance, but have risen with it. In the 1980s there were some 50,000 temps in the UK; by the mid 2010s, there were 270,000. Temps can be taken on to meet gaps in the workforce, allowing companies to speed up or slow down production at the level of hiring and firing. Some temps are even hired on an hourly basis.[11] The temp is precarious. When she does have a contract, this is without the rights of a full permanent employee. She is expected to be flexible, to undertake a variety of tasks, moving quickly, even seamlessly between them. She has already incurred the costs of training. She must quickly apprehend and work with the emotional landscape of her new workplace.

This pattern of moving between temporary positions is replacing securer Fordist jobs for many workers. Most of the new jobs created tend to be low-paid service work: between 2010 and 2013, for example, four out of five of the jobs created

9   Lynne Pettinger, *What's Wrong with Work?* (Bristol & Chicago: Policy Press, 2019), p. 99.
10   See Catherine Casey & Petricia Alach, '"Just a temp?" Women, temporary employment and lifestyle', *Work, Employment & Society*, vol. 18, no. 3, September 2004, pp. 459–80.
11   Pettinger, *What's Wrong with Work*, p. 100.

were low-paid.[12] The service sector makes up nearly 80% of the UK's economy.[13] Now, Covid-19 puts these jobs, which tend to be in retail and hospitality, at further risk. This means an increasingly polarised workforce, with a small number of people holding secure work, some of which is subjectively fulfilling, too, while the rest of the workforce provides services to those workers. There are, however, some caveats to this story. Firstly, as sociologist Lynne Pettinger reminds us,

> [p]aid work has always had precarious elements if you look beyond the labour aristocracy of unionised (male) manufacturing in countries with decent welfare state settlements. Day labouring has long been common in construction; agricultural work relies on desperate seasonal workers; domestic service workers are vulnerable to being dismissed (without employer references) if they don't show respect or respectability. So, in the glorious days of full employment and good working lives, there were many without protection, both those in and outside of formal employment.[14]

While precarity is on the rise, we shouldn't imagine contemporary work as representing a total rupture with the past. Secondly, not everyone was horribly, unbearably bored under Fordism. Working – a temporary stage between an artificially shortened education and marriage – often provided a sense of community, friendship, and even fun alongside their wages for young working-class women. And thirdly, it is important not

---

12   https://tuc.org.uk/news/four-five-jobs-created-june-2010-have-been-low-paid-industries (last accessed December 2020).

13   https://ft.com/content/2ce78f36-ed2e-11e5-888e-2eadd5fbc4a4 (last accessed December 2020).

14   Pettinger, *What's Wrong with Work*, p. 107.

to overstate the 'fun-ness' of 'new work'. In practice, new fun, ephemeral gimmicks do little to change what people actually *do* in their roles. Even in the shimmer of co-working spaces, many companies hire entire floors and function like a traditional office. Once start-ups become more established, older hierarchies, never having really gone away, re-establish themselves, both formally and informally.

Measuring changes things: neoliberalism and perverse incentives

The neoliberal policies that heralded the end of Fordism didn't just promise the end of boring work; they promised the end of bureaucracy and the introduction of fast-moving, all-night-long, friction-free capitalism. There is, then, an irony about what happened next. Rather than doing away with restrictions, a growing and deepening layer of bureaucracy emerged within previously public institutions. Two-thirds of UK universities now hire more administrative staff than they do academics. In the US, between 1975 and 2008, the number of faculty grew about 10% while the number of administrators grew 221%.[15]

Initially, this seems puzzling. This bureaucratic bulk seems to be the sort of thing that 'unleashing the power of business' would obliterate. However, the related processes of privatising and marketising require a great deal of effort. As Mark Fisher puts it:

[t]he idealised market was supposed to deliver 'friction free' exchanges, in which the desires of consumers would be met directly, without the need for intervention or mediation by

---

15   https://theguardian.com/commentisfree/2017/aug/21/universities-broke-cut-pointless-admin-teaching (last accessed December 2020).

regulatory agencies. Yet the drive to assess the performance of workers and to measure forms of labour which, by their nature, are resistant to quantification, has inevitably required additional layers of management and bureaucracy.[16]

This effort is just as much a matter of cajoling existing employees into accepting new, leaner work processes, accepting their fate as neoliberal subjects, as it is about the creation of new standards of comparison. To introduce a market into something that was previously a publicly owned monopoly requires the creation of new processes for capturing, storing, comparing and acting on data. Moreover, the capture of data in the first place changes the kind of work that even those not directly hired to work with that data do. Consider teaching. How do you record data on something so inherently relational and reciprocal? The first step is to change the tasks involved in a given job so that they can actually be recorded. Measuring something changes it. In the case of universities, for example, one metric for measuring the 'success' of teaching, is student feedback surveys. These surveys ask students whether they enjoyed a module. There is not always a straightforward link between having enjoyed something and having learned something. What is being measured here is something other than teaching. In Fisher's words, '[w]hat we have is not a direct comparison of workers' performance or output, but a comparison between the audited representation of that performance and output. Inevitably, a short circuiting occurs, and work becomes geared towards the generation and massaging of representations'.[17] In this way, neoliberalism creates perverse incentives. Instead of doing the stated tasks of a job, more and more time is spent recording

16   Mark Fisher, *Capitalist Realism* (Winchester: Zero Books, 2009), p. 41.
17   Ibid.

partial or totally one-sided representations of that work. These are then used to shape the parameters of the future conditions and terms of that same job. In doing so, it creates a new reality, through distortion.

The main focus of thinking about the perverse incentives that marketisation and privatisation bring about has been higher education. This is, perhaps, unsurprising, as most of the people writing about marketisation, or at least most of those paid to do so, are academics. Academics also tend to have a clear sense of marketisation as in contradiction to the kind of activity – non-instrumental, perhaps even 'a calling' – that they see themselves as doing. Sometimes, you get the feeling that academics think they're a special case, or that they're the only part of the economy in which a workforce has been disciplined by neoliberalism. However, they're not. It's worth investigating how marketisation and privatisation are playing out in the rest of the economy and how this affects the experience of modern work.

The experience of 'New Work'

In the last decades of the twentieth century, sections of the British economy that were previously publicly owned were sold off. This included Britoil, British Telecom, British Aerospace, British Gas, Rolls-Royce, British Rail and regional water authorities, among others. The selling-off of key industries and public services remains unpopular with the general public, the majority of whom support public ownership for rail, mail, buses and energy.[18]

---

18 https://weownit.org.uk/public-solutions/support-public-ownership (last accessed December 2020).

With the railways, awareness of the significant subsidy that the government pays to private companies to run public services strengthens the call for renationalisation. Subsidies for the railways cost all of us £5 billion per year – before we've even paid ticket prices – an increase of 200% since their privatisation.[19] The Covid-19 pandemic has meant that Westminster has announced that the railway franchise system will be wound up, but this doesn't mean an end to privatisation. Instead, a new privatised system, possibly involving concessions, in which train companies are paid a fixed fee, already in place on parts of the rail network, will come into force.[20]

Unlike in the US where private companies step in to fill the gap left by a welfare state never having really been built, in the UK, private companies deliver previously public services. The services remain free at the point of use (with the exception of dentistry), but many are run by private companies. The performance of the companies running these services is monitored by the body that would have originally provided the service themselves – national and local government, local NHS structures and so on. The process of outsourcing, of paying private companies to carry out the work of public services, accelerated in the 1980s with the introduction of 'compulsory competitive tendering'. This legislation placed a requirement on public sector organisations to tender all contracts for service delivery, meaning that anyone could bid for them. The contract was awarded to the company that would provide the service the most cheaply. This duty was relaxed slightly in 1997 but by then outsourcing was established as the new normal. Now, £284 billion per year is spent buying goods and services from external

---

19   https://fullfact.org/economy/how-much-does-government-subsidise-railways/ (last accessed December 2020).

20   https://bbc.co.uk/news/business-54232015 (last accessed December 2020).

suppliers. This is about a third of all of public expenditure[21] and 13% of GDP.[22]

These contracts are not only a huge part of the government budget, they are also employers of hundreds of thousands of people. Finding exact figures on the number of people employed by these outsourcing companies to carry out public contract work is difficult. We do know that because of outsourcing and privatisation, between 1979 and 1991, the number of people employed in public sector corporations fell by more than 1.5 million. Serco – a company that provides a variety of contracts for public services to local and national government and NHS trusts, including housing asylum seekers – employs 30,000 people in the UK. G4S employs 25,000.

I want to return to the trends – precarity, flexibility, affectivity, decentralisation, polarisation – identified earlier, in order to consider how they play out in subcontracted, formerly public, employment. What is it like to work under these conditions? To find out, I attended a branch meeting of the RMT trade union. The RMT represents 80,000 workers in the transport sector. Although most privatised railways are operated under the franchise model, in which each operation is a discrete private business, many ostensibly publicly owned sections of the network maintain private involvement through the use of concessions to provide some (or all) of their services. Concessions differ from the standard rail franchising model in which a private company generates revenue directly from rail fares. In a concession, a large sum of money is paid by the public sector to manage the operation on its behalf, including the employment

21 https://instituteforgovernment.org.uk/summary-government-procurement-scale-nature-contracting-uk (last accessed December 2020).

22 https://theguardian.com/business/2018/jul/09/carillion-collapse-exposed-government-outsourcing-flaws-report (last accessed December 2020).

of staff. In the concession model, the private company runs the service in return for a fee and is subject to more specific contractual obligations. The most comprehensive example of this is Transport for London, which owns and operates London Underground directly, but contracts private companies to run all other arms of the business, for example, London Overground, Docklands Light Railway, TfL Rail and London Buses, as concessions. The advantages to TfL are obvious – none of the privately operated concessions offer comparable rates of pay to London Underground and large liabilities such as pension pots are kept off TfL's books. Sensitive to the unpopularity of rail privatisation, the presence of private operators (almost always owned by the same foreign states that own the franchises) is kept hidden from public view.

Privatised railways use concessions to provide some of its services. In the concession model, the company runs the service in return for a fee and is subject to more specific contractual obligations. The workers at the branch meeting I attended work for a railway concession in the South East of England. In addition to the concession, two further subcontractors provide facilities management and cleaning services. Often these complex contracting and subcontracting structures don't really affect an organisation's bottom line, although they may actually add to the overall expense by creating parallel or duplicate bureaucratic structures. They divide the workforce, making it harder for workers to organise. The added cost of paying agency fees more than makes up for the advantage of keeping the most precarious and low paid sections of the workforce contractually separate from the core group of employees.

Trade unions are organisations that advocate for the rights of workers at work. A union, at least at the level of a branch meeting, can be something like a project of translation. Members present their everyday problems, and these are translated by reps or collectively transformed in meetings into something more concretely political. The material stuff of everyday work – delays in getting uniforms, access to cooking facilities and mess rooms, or the lack of heaters – becomes visible as a question of politics, and a question of work.

As Raymond Williams tells us: '[m]ost work can only be done if its means are provided: tools, materials, workplaces, outlets. But then the decision about what work will actually have to be done and how falls to those who own or control those means. The means of work have passed into the hands of the minority who own this necessary capital'.[23] When these everyday concerns are revealed, through collective translation, as political questions, they can become questions that get to the heart of work, that put pressure on the conditions under which it is carried out. At the branch meeting, many of these concerns could be related back to the demands placed on workers within contemporary work practices, in particular, the demand of affectivity, of having a friendly customer-service attitude. Just like in marketised higher education, on privatised rail, 'customer experience' is king. Customer satisfaction, however, does not mean a better service. What it does mean is that workers are expected to smile all the time, to greet 'customers' (passengers) within ten seconds of seeing them. It also means hiring people from non-rail backgrounds, from senior management down, making it easier to enact huge changes in workplace culture with limited resistance. This effort to break the 'bad habits' (read: trade union membership) ingrained into experienced railway workers also succeeds in importing high staff turnover and low morale typical of the precarious workplace culture they are trying to emulate.

---

23 Fraser, *Work*, pp. 294–5.

While many 'jobs for life' were abolished through the destruction of whole industries, the traditionally high staff retention on the railway has been eroded through attrition rather than demolition.

Within the privatised and marketised public sector, branding is key. Never mind that in the majority of cases, people have no real choice over which service to use (you have to get a specific train to work, the nearest hospital is the one you're most likely to use), market ideology means everyone and everything must be aware of and always improving their brand identity. This has an effect on the material stuff of everyday work. You have to wear, wait for, and wash branded uniforms. Once, on a station visit from their head office, one of the concession directors insisted all agency staff take off their (shamefully unbranded) gloves. The brand is expressed through positive customer interactions. These are checked by 'mystery shoppers', gig economy workers paid to use services and report to the company on the service they receive, with the company monitoring these measured and ritualised processes centrally.

Concessions are supposed to do away with the inefficiencies of franchises by stipulating specific key performance indicators (KPIs) and fining concession-runners when these are not met. These KPIs – intended to steer and manage workers – create perverse incentives. One KPI stipulates that there must always be a train-time sign working on every station. If even one side is broken, the concession-runner will be fined. This means that a worker must stand beneath the train time board and provide information on train times to passengers to mitigate the fine, even if the other side of the board is working fine, or another board is clearly visible. The train is run to the performance indicators, maximising profit, even if it negatively impacts the service in some other way. This is strikingly clear in an issue one RMT rep raised with me: if they have a late train, they must frequently cancel stops at smaller stations to make up time and avoid the fine, even if that means leaving five or ten passengers sitting on a platform for half an hour extra.

The paradox of the apparent decentralisation of new work, with its hidden deeper concentration of power within it, is particularly clear in how the concession's management have taken the spontaneous and emotional and routinised them. A particularly illuminating example is the quote boards at station entrances. A few years ago, workers in a London Tube station decided, of their own accord, to write quotes on the service updates whiteboard in their ticket hall. The quotes were a mixture of the sentimental, the humorous, the earnest, the capital I-inspirational, and occasionally, the genuinely moving. People took pictures of the board and shared them on social media. On the concession in question, this spontaneity is transformed into a central directive: each station is emailed the same quote ready for the next morning, these are written on the whiteboard and then must be posted on the concession's internal app as proof of their existence. For the sovereign customer, the appearance of spontaneity remains, but beneath the surface the vampiric tendencies of capitalism (as Marx described them) bubble away.

Workers are expected to act as an emotional buffer, smoothing over passenger concerns and must appear to do so voluntarily. As they are not trusted to do this themselves, they are expected to follow scripts and are tested on them. Ticket inspectors, for example, are all asked to direct a passenger to the same location, the British Museum. This bizarre customer service ritual is repeated daily. Even though the same question is asked each day, and the answer presumably known by heart, the worker is expected to go through the pretence of looking up the answer. To make matters even more ridiculous, the process has been literally gamified: an interactive game designed to show workers how to relay travel instructions has been developed. The underlying message of these rituals is that workers need to be remade, shown how to do their job better, in the interests of a rather nebulous 'customer service'.

In its expanded use of flexible agency staff, in its deep emotional demands, in its routinised pseudo-spontaneity and sociability, in its creation of perverse incentives, this concession's work practices are paradigmatic of changes to conditions of work in the last few decades. This reality stands against the myth of the gradual progress of work; against the claim that it is becoming more humane. It is not necessarily better or worse in terms of any one individual's experience, which would be hard to measure, given that this would be subjective. However, it is possible to say that the emotional demands placed on workers, alongside the precarity and lack of control over their time at work, and their time in general, further problematise the idea of continuously improving working lives. In fact, as the concession shows, the arcane and ritualised customer service practices that shape a great deal of contemporary work leave people detached from the tasks their jobs involve or should involve, and from their own selves. No wonder so many of today's workers are so miserable.

Chapter 4

What does work do to us as individuals?

The history of your body is the history of these names, one after, another, destroying you. The history of your body stands as an *accusation*. – Edouard Louis[1]

Work in the abstract seems capable of bringing pleasure. We can find joy in the effort we expend making something, caring for someone, or even just in the rhythm of repetitive tasks. In fact, in a phenomenon dubbed the 'Ikea effect' after the Swedish flatpack furniture stores, we tend to value objects we've made ourselves more highly. But pleasures of effort are not distributed fairly within work under capitalism. The same is true of the meaning and recognition that work can provide. Because so much of our time is spent at work, our ability to find alternative sources of joy or meaning are reduced, too. In our jobs, the extent to which we can find enjoyment or fulfilment is shaped by how much control we have over our work.

Of course, some jobs are generally considered to be worse than others. That is, they have worse or more harmful effects on those employed in them. They might confer a low status, they might involve heavy labour, they might be dangerous but not

---

1 Edouard Louis, *Who Killed my Father* (London: Harvill Secker, 2019), p. 79.

considered heroic, they might be repetitive. Abattoir work, for example, fits all of these categories. A woman who worked in a slaughterhouse for six years describes her experience:

> Soon, though, I realised there was no point pretending that it was just another job. I'm sure not all abattoirs are the same but mine was a brutal, dangerous place to work. There were countless occasions when, despite following all of the procedures for stunning, slaughterers would get kicked by a massive, spasming cow as they hoisted it up to the machine for slaughter. [. . .]
>
> Personally, I didn't suffer physical injuries, but the place affected my mind. As I spent day after day in that large, windowless box, my chest felt increasingly heavy and a grey fog descended over me. At night, my mind would taunt me with nightmares, replaying some of the horrors I'd witnessed throughout the day.[2]

Work can be extremely physiologically dangerous, for example, in the case of jobs that involve dangerous chemicals, like the carbon disulphide released when the synthetic fabric rayon is produced, or the asbestos used to insulate buildings. Shift work – when workers are employed outside of regular 9-5 hours, and often through the night – can cause serious cardiovascular problems, as well as being linked to anxiety and depression.[3] Delivery work can make workers vulnerable to traffic accidents or threats of violence, particularly when this work is carried out alone and under intense time pressure.[4]

---

2   https://bbc.co.uk/news/stories-50986683 (last accessed December 2020).
3   https://oem.bmj.com/content/58/1/68 (last accessed December 2020).
4   Callum Cant, *Riding for Deliveroo* (Cambridge: Polity Press, 2019), p. 54.

The problem of work is often seen as a problem of the distribution of this kind of harmful job. Some jobs are dirty or difficult or happen at odd times, but someone has to do them; it's unfortunate that someone has to take the hit, and perhaps they ought to be better compensated. This way of categorising work misses something important. Such cases are more extreme than others, but the difference is of degree, not of kind. All of our jobs have significant effects on our health, on our relationships with ourselves and our relationships with others.

Construction work has a particularly high rate of workplace injuries. It can cause hearing loss, breathing problems and lung disease, skin conditions and back injuries. In Britain in the financial year 2018/19, there were 30 fatal workplace injuries in the construction sector and 54,000 non-fatal injuries.[5] But it's not just work that is typically considered manual that can cause physiological injury – the health and care sector saw 74,000 injuries in the same year.[6] The work of lifting and supporting human bodies in care work is physical and can be dangerous. Cleaning can be dangerous too: a survey of Danish full-time cleaners found that 20% experienced daily pain as a result of their work.[7] Even the kind of work often termed 'immaterial'[8] involves moving and manipulating our bodies: office workers sit at desks all day long, often with poorly aligned chairs and desks; serving staff in the food industry are on their feet all day,

---

5   https://hse.gov.uk/statistics/industry/construction.pdf (last accessed December 2020).

6   https://hse.gov.uk/statistics/industry/health.pdf (last accessed December 2020).

7   Karen Søgaard, Anne Katrine Blangsted, Andrew Herod & Lotte Finsen, 'Work Design and the Labouring Body: Examining the Impacts of Work Organization on Danish Cleaners' Health' in *Cleaners and the Dirty Work of Neoliberalism*, Luis L.M. Aguiar and Andrew Herod, (Oxford: Blackwell Publishing, 2006), p. 150.

8   See Michael Hardt and Antonio Negri, *Empire* (Cambridge, MA: Harvard University Press, 2000).

with little time to eat their own meals; operating checkout tills can cause musculoskeletal injuries and problems, particularly to backs, shoulders and arms.[9] Repetitive motions, whether on the factory production line or at an office, can have damaging effects on the human body. Foxconn factory workers – who produce half the world's iPhones and many other Apple products – report that they make the motions required of them during their job, involuntarily while not at work.[10]

As well as physical stress, work can cause psychological difficulties for workers too. Though we shouldn't draw too sharp a line between mental and physical health, the two are interwoven. The available data on the harms that work can cause, however, does distinguish between the two. The assumption of a mind/body divide is unfortunate and unhelpful, but we've got to work with the statistics we have. Those statistics are pretty damning: workload pressure is the single greatest cause of work-related illness in the UK. 12.7% of all sickness absence days in the UK can be attributed to mental health conditions.[11] These problems are not external to the workplace; they are often exacerbated by conditions at work. One helpful way of understanding work pressure is to consider it in terms of 'work intensity' – the expectations of what you're supposed to produce in a given time frame – and overtime work – hours outside of regular contracted hours. Both are factors in workers' stress and fatigue.[12] Unpaid

9   https://usdaw.org.uk/CMSPages/GetFile.aspx?guid=b9406bec-93b2-44b3-b6f0-25edd63e137c (last accessed December 2020).

10   https://telegraph.co.uk/finance/china-business/7773011/A-look-inside-the-Foxconn-suicide-factory.html (last accessed December 2020).

11   ONS (2014). Full Report: Sickness Absence on the Labour Market, February 2014. Retrieved from webarchive.

12   http://openaccess.city.ac.uk/20071/1/avgoustaki_frankort_ILRR.pdf (last accessed December 2020).

overtime made £32.7 billion for employers in 2019.[13] On top of this time, work emails and WhatsApps from managers nibble into our evenings. According to one study, workers spent an average of eight hours a week replying to work-related emails outside of work.[14] As the director of the think tank Autonomy, Will Stronge, puts it, 'communications technology has dissolved the boundary between contracted and non-contracted hours.'[15] These deeper and longer patterns of working only compound existing stress and mental ill-health.

Control and the illusion of choice

Often, overexertion at work can look like the choice of individual workers. Sometimes people stay longer to be seen to be working longer, or work faster to be seen to be working harder. This might seem like something people do of their own volition. It might even feel like a free choice. However, for many employees, the pressure to be seen to care about work can be very intense. To work according to your contracted duties, to master the tasks you are expected to do and be content enough to do them is seen as a form of slacking off in the modern workplace. We are expected to be improving, getting better, treating everyone as a customer, improving our processes, reflecting, appraising, reviewing, changing, without stop.

While in hyper-competitive workplaces this feeling can be stoked by competition between employees, it is usually encouraged by management. Our employers have two forms of

13   https://tuc.org.uk/news/workers-uk-put-more-%C2%A332-billion-worth-unpaid-overtime-last-year-tuc-analysis (last accessed December 2020).

14   https://theguardian.com/commentisfree/2020/feb/13/unpaid-electronic-labour-right-disconnect (last accessed December 2020).

15   Ibid.

control over us. Firstly, as a group, they have indirect control over our lives. We, unless we're very, very rich, must work to live. We need an employer to employ us. Secondly, we do not choose the conditions under which we work. At work, our employers have direct control over our activities. This could mean that they and only they know how the algorithms that determine who taxi drivers pick up next work, or that they set the expected hours of work, or have control over which equipment workers are given. We don't control the conditions of our work and challenging them can be difficult. Because of the background unfreedom – the fact that we are compelled to work – challenging bad workplace practices, such as not having proper safety equipment, routine unpaid overtime, even harassment and discrimination all become harder. If you need a job to live, especially if it's hard to get one (you don't have the right kinds of skills or the right permits to work, or there's high unemployment), the direct control your boss has over you is greater. You're more likely to have to go along with practices that put your or other people's health in danger – or just make you miserable – if you need the job more than the job needs you. This can also cause bullying and belittling behaviour. At the extreme end, one worker reported on an online forum that their boss insisted that all employees register as potential liver donors for his sick brother, or he would fire them.[16] In more mundane cases, workers are often hesitant to ask for adjustments or for leave. They regularly work when they're ill, either because they'll lose pay if they don't show up, or because career progression depends on being seen to be working as hard as possible.

This direct control might come from your boss, or 'team leader', through your manager, or, and increasingly, it might

---

16   https://askamanager.org/2016/04/our-boss-will-fire-us-if-we-dont-sign-up-to-be-a-liver-donor-for-his-brother.html (last accessed December 2020).

come from an algorithm that even your boss's boss doesn't have control over. In Amazon warehouses, for example, the movements of each worker are monitored constantly: how long it takes to pick an item for delivery, how often a worker spends in the toilet, and so on. These are compared to expected standards, often strenuous, like packing hundreds of boxes per hour. Not meeting the required standards can lead to workers being fired. There is often no human involvement in the administration of this process.[17] Workers are managed and even fired by algorithms. This changes the nature of control in the workplace. While it doesn't remove human input – somewhere down the line people wrote the code for the algorithm, following the instructions of other people – it does change how you relate to the tasks you are paid to do. Rather than the possibility or actuality of a manager watching you and catching you working sub-optimally, there's no place to hide. In Amazon warehouses, there are still managers, they just follow the instructions given to them by a computer. This means that appealing everyday decisions that don't make sense becomes impossible. As one worker in an Amazon warehouse put it: '[t]he AI is your boss, your boss's boss, and your boss's boss's boss: it sets the target productivity rates, the shift quotas, and the division of labour on the floor'.[18]

As outlined above, control – algorithmic or human, or some combination of the two – determines how we relate to our work and leads to situations in which our jobs can put us at risk – it becomes harder to challenge dangerous practices. But it's more than just the sum of these individual moments. This lack of control could *itself* be a cause of poor health and misery. A study

17   https://theverge.com/2019/4/25/18516004/amazon-warehouse-fulfillment-centers-productivity-firing-terminations (last accessed December 2020).

18   https://homintern.soy/posts/wemachines.html (last accessed December 2020).

of British civil servants found a close connection between rank, amount of control over daily tasks and health outcomes. We might expect that more control and higher rank would lead to more stress and therefore worse health. Being the person with whom the proverbial buck stops is generally considered to be stressful. High-powered executives take off on multiple holidays, undergo digital detoxes and visit luxury spas to cope with stress. But this study found that a civil servant of a higher grade has less of a chance of dying from lung cancer than one of a lower rank who smokes the same number of cigarettes.[19] Having control at work was the most successful single factor in explaining the threefold difference in death rates between senior and junior civil servants working in the same government offices.[20]

'Good work'

With the possibility of secure, permanent and long-term jobs eroding in the UK, the government, among others, has turned its attention to 'decent' or 'good' work. Public Health England, for example, argues that good work involves a decent wage, opportunities for development and training, flexibility to balance family life and work, and is free from hazards. They advise:

> Being in good work is better for your health than being out of work. 'Good work' is defined as having a safe and secure job with

---

19   Marmot MG, Smith GD, Stansfeld S, Patel C, North F, Head J, White I, Brunner E, Feeney A., 'Health inequalities among British civil servants: the Whitehall II study', *Lancet*, 337, 1991, pp. 387–93.

20   See Dan Swain, *Alienation* (Bookmarks, London: 2012), pp. 65–6 for a helpful discussion of what to make of these findings.

good working hours and conditions, supportive management and opportunities for training and development.[21]

While the conditions they suggest are much better than those many of today's workers find themselves in – and though we might question, given the health issues that work can cause, the possibility of a 'safe' job – they miss the crucial element of control. The question of control in work involves not only self-direction and control over conditions of the day to day tasks of work, but a reduction, or even obliteration, of the difference in power between workers (who have very little control), managers (who are delegated some day-to-day powers) and bosses (who have much more control over conditions).

One way of understanding why this lack of control over the activities of work causes such harm is through Marx's idea of 'alienation'. On his account, engaging in conscious, creative, world-creating activity is what it is to be human. This capacity is distorted under capitalism. It becomes something a dispossessed class are forced to sell to the wealthy, who own the machinery and premises where this capacity is set to work. This has a disastrous effect on human social life. The worker is unable to make sense of themselves, and the world around them, their relationships with others become instrumental, and the whole world appears as something alien:

The cellar dwelling of the poor man is a hostile element . . . a dwelling which he cannot regard as his own hearth . . . he finds himself in someone else's house, in the house of a

21   https://gov.uk/government/publications/health-matters-health-and-work/
health-matters-health-and-work (last accessed December 2020).

stranger who always watches him and throws him out if he does not pay his rent.[22]

The experience of working under conditions you do not control, producing commodities that wield power over you, for someone else's profit, is a frustration of human potential. Let's return to Public Health England's claim that '[b]eing in good work is better for your health than being out of work'. With the number of people who, despite being *in* work, live in poverty at a record high, this suggestion seems a little confused.[23] Perhaps they would argue that most available work doesn't meet the standards of 'good' work. But what about the standards of 'good' *un*employment? Being in work is only better for someone's health because of the conditions – and these are conditions that are *political* choices – that the unemployed face.

The protections for unemployed workers have been decimated by successive governments. A punitive regime of benefits sanctions and cuts, designed to 'get people back into work', whatever work, and sometimes even working for free, has destroyed the lives of thousands of people. As Rachel O'Brien, the Policy and Public Affairs Officer at Inclusion London, the London-wide Deaf and Disabled people's organisation told me:

This punitive approach has destroyed the lives of thousands of people. In some cases, this punitive system has led directly to their deaths, with Calum's List documenting the suicides that have occurred as a result of welfare reform,[24] and the

---

22   Karl Marx, *Economic and Philosophic Manuscripts of 1844* (Amherst, NY: Prometheus Books, 1988), p. 124.

23   https://theguardian.com/business/2020/feb/07/uk-live-poverty-charity-joseph-rowntree-foundation (last accessed December 2020).

24   See http://calumslist.org/ (last accessed December 2020).

Disability News Service presenting the 'Case for the Prosecution' of the Department for Work and Pensions following five years of research into the deaths of people found 'fit to work' and the alleged misconduct in public office of senior civil servants and ministers in the Department. When Disabled people do make it into the workplace, past the discrimination present in the advertising and recruitment for jobs, Disabled people are faced with widening pay gaps and are more likely to be employed on a zero-hours contract with fewer rights in the workplace.

Whether it is the retroactive ideological justification or the formative underlying ethic of cuts to the welfare state, the claim that hard work is morally good and laziness morally culpable pervades contemporary politics. To be unemployed is to have failed. In wage societies, paid work, our jobs, are the primary route through which we can gain recognition from others. As work extends over more and more of human social life, something discussed in more detail in the next chapter, possible countervailing sources of recognition – from friendship, from our hobbies, from shared social practices – dissolve. For the unemployed person, even the limited, class-stratified and instrumental recognition possible within capitalist work is lost.

Work, inequality, and shame

Work affords us a degree of recognition, a feeling of being seen for who we take ourselves to be and a chance to be appreciated by our fellow humans. It also changes how we interact with the world and with others. If you've worked waiting tables, you know that plates are usually served from the left and cleared from the right. When you're eating at a restaurant you might even instinctively lean to your left or right to make your waiter's task simpler. In this way, it's not just physiology that work changes. While your arms and wrists might strengthen from carrying multiple plates, and the skin on your hands grow alarmingly impervious to extremes of temperature, being a waiter also changes your orientation in a given environment. Our knowledge of and orientations within workplaces are shaped by the work we do. A cleaner will navigate a workplace, and indeed the world at large, differently to a senior manager: knowing your place is a spatial as much as it is a psychological phenomenon.

Those in jobs marked out as 'lower' status (unskilled manual labour, 'dirty' work, routine service work, among others) are denied access to the meaning, autonomy, and recognition of higher status work. The sociologist Richard Sennett terms this lack of status and the psychological fallout from it the 'hidden injuries of class'. In a class society, he argues, not everyone is given 'secure dignity' in the eyes of others. This is because someone's class position is 'presented as the ultimate outcome of personal ability', and because attempts to legitimise the self in that same society are likely to fail, and therefore, to 'reinforce the original anxiety'.[25] Even when someone travels upwards between classes, the lingering feeling of status anxiety, he argues, remains. While this anxiety and suffering permeate across human social life, it is directly encountered at work. Those of lower rank are instructed, managed and monitored by those 'above' them. Not only are they treated *instrumentally*, but this instrumentality, and the subservient forms it takes, hail their lower status.

Two incidents in my early life showed me how these differences in status have profound effects. The first of these was witnessing a fight between two women outside of my primary school. One

---

25   Richard Sennett and Jonathan Cobb, *The Hidden Injuries of Class* (New York & London: Norton & Company,1993), p. 171.

of the women worked in the school's reception, and, as was revealed during the fight, she also worked as a cleaner for the other woman, a mother collecting her children. I had assumed they were friends because they were often together. In the same way that adults assume that children have uncomplicated and easy friendships, children tend to assume that adults who act as if they are friends truly are. During this fight, the second woman retorted, 'well, you clean my toilets'. This statement shocked every eavesdropper in a ten-metre radius, reverberating round the school for days. It showed, in an instant, the contempt for those with low-status work, even by those who have themselves produced the dirt that the workers were hired to clean. The second was being awarded, at age eleven, a means-tested bursary to a private school. I went from membership of the group least likely to make it to university – recipients of free school meals – to the group whose future is set in gilded stone. This kind of class travelling is unnerving when it happens to fully grown adults; for children it is a disorienting and lonely initiation into a world of unearned and ill-deserved privilege. When you take a child who has grown up poor and put them in an environment where they are not only surrounded by the very rich but also there as a charity case, the explicit and implicit contours of class quickly become visible to them: it's not just a case of how much you own (although the rest tends to be downstream of this), but of how you are taught to carry yourself, of what you are expected to believe of yourself, and how you are taught to look down on those of 'lower' status. Class is a mechanism that permits some people to make themselves heard but enforces silence on others, denying them power and agency. The language of class is also a language of particular work – middle-class professionals talk in an argot that is impenetrable and often technocratically dehumanising when it comes to those of lower status. The ability to use this language, to talk in terms of 'outcomes' and 'going-forwards' and 'as-per-my-previous-emails', are a particular set of professional soft skills, which give those who possess them the ability to move more easily between jobs and to gain status and material support in times of hardship.

The division of labour, with some jobs coded as more worthy of respect and dignity than others, is a source of significant harm. But for those pushed out of it, either temporarily or more permanently, it is not just income lost but a major site of social esteem. This means significant marginalisation on multiple fronts. That our jobs are one of the only places in which people can express themselves is a travesty. It's not that people should not find fulfilment in work but, given the time demands that work places on most people, and the destruction of and cuts to other sources of meaning and fulfilment, there are only rare chances for other moments of fulfilment. Those who cannot work or cannot find work, especially those who are poor, are excluded from society. This is particularly true given the 'shirkers vs strivers' rhetoric of governments and the mainstream press, which puts forward working as coterminous with membership of community.[26] In this way, exclusion from work becomes doubly violent, another hidden injury of class, wherein a structural societal problem is presented as an individual failing. The kinds of conditionality imposed on benefits as well as the reduction in the total available amount might achieve the goal of 'making work pay' but only relative to an artificially created state of deepening poverty and exclusion.

Work 'pays' when wages rise, not when the floor for those outside of it is lowered. This cruel system creates a social layer below those in work, even in crap work. The writer Kerry

---

26   Mareile Pfannebecker, J. A. Smith, *Work Want Work* (London: Zed Books, 2020), p. 30.

Hudson describes her experience of growing up in this stratum, among poverty that was 'all-encompassing, grinding, brutal and often dehumanising', as one that formed 'the bones, the blood and muscle, the very substance of me'. The psychic injuries of class lingered despite her success as a novelist; '[w]hen every day of your life you have been told you have nothing of value to offer, that you are worth nothing to society, can you ever escape that sense of being "lowborn" no matter how far you've come?'[27] Political attacks on working-class institutions, including trade unions, means there are fewer ways through which the privatisation of societal problems can be challenged, politically and interpersonally. The injuries of unfair access to recognition and meaning, and the self-blame that come with them, can remain hidden, the secret possessions of isolated individuals.

In many lines of work, harassment and being spoken down to are so common as to be practically part of the job description. This is particularly the case in the gendered and racialised service sector. If our physiological and spatial orientations are affected by our working days, what about our sense of self? What effect might daily repetition of the gendered and deferential patterns of speech and movement that service work demands have on our self-esteem and our lives outside of work?

According to sociologist Arlie Hochschild, the demands placed on our personalities and selves in the expectation that we produce and manage emotional states on demand, ought to be concerning. The 'separation' of the worker's 'face' and 'feeling' is 'potentially estranging.'[28] Our feelings are treated as 'raw ore'.[29]

---

27 Kerry Hudson, *Lowborn* (Random House: eBook, 2019).

28 Arlie Hochschild, *The Managed Heart* (Berkeley & New York: University of California Press, 2012), p. 35.

29 Ibid., p. 54.

When we are called upon to manage or produce emotional states as part of our jobs, the expectation that our personality is also raw material is entrenched. Work makes intense demands on us. Through work, our bodily – physical, mental, and emotional – capacities are used for profit. This happens under conditions we have very little say over. In a service-heavy economy, we are increasingly called upon to deploy more and more of ourselves – our personalities – for our employers.

With the possibilities for long-term, secure, permanent and well-paid work decreasing, work creeps in several directions. We work harder at work. We work longer hours. At work, we are expected to use our emotions and personalities for the benefit of our employers. Outside of our official working hours, we are called upon to excavate more of our social lives, turning hobbies into side gigs so that we can survive on our current jobs' meagre salaries and scrape enough social and cultural capital or resources to get another job in the future.

It's not just contingent bad practices that make work harmful. Nor is it just the persistence of a few bad jobs. While work can be dangerous, exploitative or even just boring, *all* work under capitalism harms workers because of the coercion that pushes us into it, and the lack of control we face during it.

Chapter 5

Jobification nation: When play is serious business

A popular image has been circulating online for the past few years. A simple black and white outline of a rose adorned with text proclaiming that 'you are worth so much more than your productivity'. The image, made by Instagram user and designer @radicalemprints, went viral, or as viral as left-leaning memes can go, in 2015.[1] If you're in any radical online spaces, it's likely that you'll have seen it or seen a version of it. The intention of the image is to call into question the attachment of one's self-worth to how much work one does or trappings of external success. That we measure ourselves against standards we can't meet because there is always, theoretically, more we could be doing, is a real source of pain and frustration. The claim, 'you are worth so much more than your productivity' is an attempt to reimagine what value is or what a person's worth could be. The limitation of this kind of thinking is that while reconfiguring our individual attitudes can act as a balm against a person's feelings of inadequacy or failure, they do little, usually, to address the reality that your socially measured worth and your productivity, at work or for future work, are related. Without building durable

---

1   https://instagram.com/p/B6ZsjxiAvF-/ (last accessed December 2020).

and shared sites of worth outside of market relations, we are stuck with the valuation of worth as productivity.

Why is it that productivity has such a pull for so many of us? We find ourselves looking for that final hack that will set our day right, allow us to speed through our growing to-do-lists, plan for the future but not to sweat the small things, rise and grind, and so on. We might feel that we simply have too much to do and not enough time to do it in. This feeling is not in and of itself a new phenomenon: worries about the impossibility of doing everything someone should do, such as read all the right kinds of things, are ancient, dating back to at least the philosopher Seneca.

Complaints of nervous exhaustion and neurasthenia in the eighteenth and nineteenth centuries respectively prefigure today's 'burnt-out' society. In 1733, George Cheyne's *The English Malady* linked city living and the pace of modern life to the problem of weak nerves. Weak nerves, he argued, meant the body was unable to properly circulate vital fluids, causing lowness of spirits, lethargic dullness and melancholy.[2] While an excess of the pleasures of civilisation were behind Cheyne's malady, the nervous ailments of the late nineteenth and early twentieth centuries were caused not by excess but delicate oversensitivity to external stimuli, a sensory overload caused by, among others, the periodical press, steam power, too much brain work, or, in the case of women, any brain work. Neurasthenia, like today's burnout, was for high-flyers, with writers like Virginia Woolf and Marcel Proust known to have suffered from the illness.[3] While contemporary corporate burnout is treated with luxury spa retreats and mindfulness sessions typically costing thousands

---

2 Anna Katharina Schaffner, *Exhaustion: a History* (New York: Columbia University Press, 2016), pp. 87–90.

3 Ibid., p. 96.

of pounds, female neurasthenics were subjected to what was known as the 'rest cure'. Patients were kept in bed for weeks, in some cases, not being permitted to turn or roll without medical assistance and fed vast quantities of bland food. The removal of any stimuli, including reading or writing was the goal,[4] a particularly extreme form of rest. Like neurasthenia, burnout is seen as an ennobling affliction. It was first used to describe emotional exhaustion from social or other caring work, as in the Maslach Burnout Inventory survey developed during the 1980s for those who, according to its developer, Christina Malasch, do '"people work" of some kind'.[5] More recently, its scope has expanded, encompassing work which is less obviously to do with caring. Its more recent connotations, in mainstream discussions of exhaustion, still retain a relationship to care, but the problem becomes an excess of care exhibited by very conventionally successful people, rather than 'lower-status' social workers, nurses, and so on. This is how American magazine, *Psychology Today*, defined burnout in 2011: 'Burnout is a cunning thief that robs the world of its best and its brightest by feeding on their energy, enthusiasm, and passion, transforming these positive qualities into exhaustion, frustration, and disillusionment.'[6]

When people experience pain, sickness, or poor health, their experience is shaped by the ways in which the society they live in makes sense of their physical sensations. The expected script for poor health determines the way they experience it as well as the care they are likely to receive. Depression and burnout have a very similar set of symptoms. The WHO's International

---

4   A famous example of this can be found in *The Yellow Wallpaper* by Charlotte Perkins Gillman.

5   Schaffner, *Exhaustion*, p. 124.

6   https://psychologytoday.com/gb/blog/high-octane-women/201104/overcoming-burnout (last accessed December 2020).

Classification of Diseases notes three dimensions of burnout, 1) energy depletion or exhaustion, 2) mental distance, feelings of negativity or cynicism, and 3) a sense of ineffectiveness and lack of accomplishment.[7] Depression is similarly characterised by a lack of energy, a reduction in interest or engagement, and by low self-esteem. Burnout, however, is, at least in the WHO's definition, an 'occupational phenomenon'. On some readings, including *Psychology Today*'s, burnout is something exclusive to not only the workplace but to particular kinds of workplaces; historically, to ones that rely on emotional effort and care, but increasingly to prestigious, high-pressure corporate office work. While depression remains stigmatised, burnout's connection to professional duty and to success allows people to identify with it without social sanction.[8] Rather than the failure of will, the failure to care for oneself, which depression is often (wrongly) taken to be, burnout sufferers are the victims of an excess of care, of caring too much about their work, either because it directly involves care or because corporate life requires its high-fliers to *care* above all else about their work.

Exhaustion itself is not new. The feeling of there being just too much to do and the pre-emptive exhaustion this is bound up with is tied necessarily to the unmooring of fixed and rigid roles and hierarchies of rank that characterise capitalist modernity. If we're free to be or to do anything we want, our failure to succeed can feel, especially in competitive and highly individualised societies, like our own fault. However, the feeling that we ought to be working all the time, and not just that we should be busy or that modernity is overly stimulating, seems to be a particularly contemporary concern.

---

7   https://icd.who.int/browse11/l-m/en#/http://id.who.int/icd/entity/129180281 (last accessed December 2020).

8   Schaffner, *Exhaustion*, p. 216.

Part of the reason for this is that the relative lack of power of workers compared to employers allows for employers to push the duty of improvement, required to keep turning profits, onto workers. The self-exploitation that characterises the experience of contemporary capitalist work is not just a source of individual misery but a means of guaranteeing profit. Alongside a dizzyingly rapid growth in inequality, there has been a massive transference of risk in society, moving it from the wealthy and powerful, whose profits are guaranteed even when they fail to deliver, to the poor. We can see this transference of risk at a national level, when private companies that deliver public services are bailed out at the expense of the public, or when landlords' 'investments' are protected at the risk of renters' homes. At the level of the firm, it is in the massive growth in the use of temporary and zero-hour contracts, offering flexibility that typically benefits the employer at the expense of the worker. Such contracts allow workers, rather than employers, to absorb potential costs of lost work or reduced demand. They make it cheaper to fire workers and increase the arbitrary power employers have over workers who report being unable to turn down shifts for fear of having their work reduced. With so much risk transferred down, it's no wonder that there is a widespread feeling of compulsion for self-improvement.

The cult of continuous improvement

While the WHO might feel able to easily separate out work and life with burnout as an occupational hazard, this easy cleavage runs counter to the experience of most everyday life. In place of the time-bounded work that characterised the mood of Fordism, work and leisure feel increasingly intertwined. Firstly, as we saw in Chapter 3, work makes the kinds of demands on us that leisure might historically have made: to enjoy ourselves, to be reflexive, in some cases to dress casually, to be social. Rather than work serving as a fixed time in someone's life (after education, before retirement), work has become the defining mode of their life. We are beholden not merely to an individual employer we might have at any given time, but to all future employers. Time that is not spent on some kind of improvement that will help you get a job down the line is time wasted. The productivity fixes of the last decades of the previous century were focused at the level of the firm, cutting down processes to mere, necessary bone, but today's workers are expected to exercise the scalpel on their own personalities. Productivity, once primarily a question of national statistics, becomes an ethos, guided by apps and hacks designed to make you the best possible version of yourself. Of course, this process of optimisation can yield results that are positive, that feel fulfilling, but the question of what we are self-optimising in service of can't be answered without reference to the diminishing chances of securing a job. Secondly, when it comes to leisure, two trends – the rise of data-hungry internet platforms, and the rise of so-called side gigs – compound each other to, in different ways, make our leisure more work-like.

Writing in 1951, the philosopher Theodor Adorno expressed concern about the rigid division of work and leisure, of hobbies sectioned off as outside of work, and vice versa. This division, he argued, closed off possibilities of enjoyment and fulfilment in work and of reflection in leisure. In place of this division, '[o]nly a cunning intertwining of pleasure and work [would] leave . . . real experience still open, under the pressure of society'.[9] When it came to leisure, he argued, there was a pseudo-busyness, in which '[e]verybody must have projects all the time.

---

9   Theodor Adorno, *Minima Moralia* (London and New York: Verso, 2005), p. 130.

The maximum must be extracted from leisure'. These 'projects' aren't the side gigs – the monetised hobbies, the CV-polishing, skills-accruing activities that many young people report feeling obligated to participate in today – but visits to 'every conceivable site or spectacle, or just with the fastest possible locomotion'.[10] Just as Adorno notes that these worries would be 'undreamed of' by those in years before, the problem he traces – of compulsion to externally visible busy fun in leisure, separated from work – seems outrageously outdated. Rather than a separation of work and play, play is now serious business. According to the University of Reading's Henley Business School, one in four adults in the UK have a 'side hustle' – a secondary business or job. That this is so common can be partially put down to the difficulty of finding full-time and well-paid work in an age characterised by stagnant wages and growing numbers of part-time or zero-hours posts, but this doesn't explain that 73% of people who start a 'side hustle' do so to follow a passion or explore a new challenge. Large numbers of people are approaching what we might typically imagine as work's outside, their hobbies and leisure activities, as something that could be folded into work. The most common side gigs are craft businesses, book-writing, stock market investments, buying and selling online, and blogging or vlogging.[11] 34% of 16 to 24-year-olds and 37% of 25 to 34-year-olds report having a side hustle. Of course, multiple jobs, particularly for those excluded from full time work in the formal sector, whether through gendered stereotypes, racist hiring practices, or not having the legal right to work in a country, are nothing new. Throughout capitalism's history, even in the heyday of time-bounded, secure, jobs for life, many

10   Adorno, *Minima Moralia*, p. 138.
11   https://assets.henley.ac.uk/defaultUploads/PDFs/news/Journalists-Regatta-Henley_Business_School_whitepaper_DIGITAL.pdf (last accessed December 2020).

people worked multiple jobs, straddling the formal and informal economy. While this balance between the side and the main gig can and does shift across different periods of capitalism, what is really significant to this moment is not just the amount of time spent on side gigs, or hustles, or second jobs, but that hobbies and interests are approached as something that could be or even *should* be monetised. This is the jobification of everyday life.

Identity curation and social media

Around 70% of adults in the UK have a social media account. Of every five minutes spent online, one minute is spent on social media. Even though there are age restrictions on social media platforms, around half of 12-year-olds have a social media profile.[12] More than half the world uses social media, but they use it in different ways. Some maintain shades of anonymity, or keep their profiles private, updating their close friends on what they're doing. For others, particularly the young and aspirational, social media becomes a way of cultivating your own identity, one in which, as theorists Mareile Pfannebecker and James A. Smith put it, your 'social media is a continuously rolling modelling portfolio, show-reel and curriculum vitae.'[13] Even for those who do not use social media for things that feel like work, or work-training, or building up your brand, on social media, our activity is itself put to work, made profitable for the platform giants, through the collection of data. Often the way young people use social media is the subject of derision, finger-wagging, 'In My Day'-ing, involving sweeping claims about the possible harms of the brave new

12   https://ofcom.org.uk/__data/assets/pdf_file/0024/149253/online-nation-summary.pdf (last accessed December 2020).

13   Mareile Pfannebecker & James A. Smith, *Work Want Work* (Zed Books, London, 2020), p. X.

world of the internet. While this moralising often gets it wrong, there are ways in which the internet is shaping social relations and power relations that are profoundly worrying. The internet, even when not used anonymously, allows people to interact more quickly than previous forms of communication. This is, in some ways, a marvel. You can keep in touch with friends half the way around the world and you can do so in ways that require less effort than ever before. The possibility of constant communication, however, of not being able to detach from the glowing screen, can be incredibly difficult when what you're seeing online is something that you find upsetting.

In fact, the term 'social media' or 'social network' is misleading; these are companies that form, as the writer Richard Seymour puts it, 'a social industry'. This industry, he argues, is 'able, through the production and harvesting of data, to objectify and quantify social life in numerical form.' While we are enjoying ourselves online, we are giving platforms all kinds of information about ourselves. It's not just an issue of privacy. It's that our social tendencies, our capacities for care and interest in others, our concern for how we might come across to others are rendered intelligible to and profitable for companies. There's nothing wrong with wanting to use social media platforms but we are encouraged to use them, to feel connected to others, to get the dopamine rush of a new notification, but all the time our capacities, desires, and actions are put to work. We might think we're interacting with our friends or other platform users but, as Seymour reminds us, we're really interacting with the platforms, 'with the machine. We write to it, and it passes on the message for us, after keeping a record of the data.'[14] While our leisure lives were once separate, at least spatially and temporally,

---

14   Richard Seymour, *The Twittering Machine* (London: The Indigo Press, 2019), p. 23.

from our working day, they form, in growing proportion, the raw material for social media platform profits.

Why, then, don't we just *not*? Why can't we get off social media? Why can we not act to protect our desires and social relations from the often-harmful effects of the online? One key problem is that the people we want to talk to and the most common ways of talking to each other are on there. Leaving means being left out. And: phones are lovely objects. They are designed to be held, to be thumbed, their interfaces are designed to keep your attention. The same is true of social media, whose apps and websites are designed to keep your attention, to keep you looking at them for as long as possible so that they can maximise their profits. But beyond that, social media is often something that we find pleasurable, even sometimes as it allows us to engage in some of our worst behaviours, ones we know are harmful to ourselves and to others. It latches onto our needs for connection, our jealousies and social anxieties, our crushes, and it not only exploits them but can come to shape our experiences of them. It is genuinely fun. The lifestyle that influencers and online entrepreneurs are able to obtain is glamorous and desirable – it's not a surprise that people want the sponsored content, offering free meals and other freebies, holidays, and even the 'authenticity' that its participants seem to display even as they claim to disavow the possibility that social media could be authentic. The perverse joy that social media users feel while scrolling through their own feed, noticing and managing how they've presented themselves to others, feeds on a curation of identity not possible for most people for most of human history.

The false promise of education

Work creeps over our leisure time, and it also extends into more of our lifetime, with more time spent in expensive training for work, and more time spent working as the possibility for retirement dwindles. All this work, or work-like activity, for a declining chance of getting a job. The most compelling example of this paradox is education. We spend more and more of our lives taking on more and more intricate training, and often huge amounts of debt, for increasingly fleeting chances of getting a secure job. Education and work have a longstanding connection. Indeed, educational institutions were often developed to train people for specific work – from monks, to teachers, to mechanics. However, the competitive, instrumental, and totalising forces of capitalism make education all the more oriented towards work.

The history of schooling is a history of exclusion. This runs very much contrary to the mythology of meritocratic education, but it's true: at each successive stage of schooling, children and young people are filtered out, with some selected for success and the others for the dung heap. For every smart, working-class child who gets ahead, there are thousands left behind. Our schooling system accelerates inequality, stacking the odds against those who've already missed out. These inequalities manifest themselves as a narrowing of possibility. Fewer and fewer options become available to working-class students. This narrowing presents itself as inevitable, natural and unprob-lematic. Reflecting on his working-class childhood, the French sociologist Didier Eribon describes this process as having the sense that '[t]hings have been arranged ahead of time', that the straws feel pre-drawn. 'Selection within the educational system' he writes 'often happens by a process of self-elimination, and that self-elimination is treated as if it were freely chosen: extended studies are for the other kinds of people'.[15]

The shedding-off of more and more students at each successive level of education helps justify why some people have better jobs

---

15   Didier Eribon, *Returning to Reims* (Penguin, London, 2019), pp. 46–7.

than others. If they wanted better jobs, they should have worked harder. What does this shedding-off look like? In the metaphors used to describe this process, terms like 'the leaky pipeline' used by commentators and charity organisations, it appears as something gentle and natural. In reality it is experienced through a more or less direct confrontation with overly disciplinarian and often inadequately supportive schools. Academies – schools run by private companies or organisations, which now make up the majority of secondary schools in England – often trade on their tough approach to discipline. In practice this means sending pupils home, to detention, or to isolation rooms for minor infractions. It's easy to be sensationalist about this. It's not the case that every single academy sends children home for forgetting to stand up when their teacher enters the room, though some do, of course. However, the combination of cuts – in England, support staff numbers fell by 14,300 between November 2016 and November 2017, according to the NEU[16] – and the rise of tougher rules does mean that students are more likely to be sent out of class, and when they are, are more likely to have their education disrupted. In isolation rooms, students are rarely given help with work, and sometimes are not given work at all. One languages teacher told me that, as a result of spending most of the previous year in isolation, one of his pupils has entered GCSE Spanish without having studied the language.

Adam, a History teacher, told me the ways in which existing inequalities are compounded by sixth form college:

More working-class students tend to work part time jobs while they study while their more middle-class classmates don't have to, and so often these class disparities can just

16   https://neu.org.uk/press-releases/neu-survey-shows-widespread-funding-and-workload-pressures-school-support-staff (last accessed December 2020).

grow over the two years they're at sixth form. Working class students are tired at college and busy after college and so don't have the time they would need to dedicate to doing their work as well as they can.

This all takes its toll on young people who report record levels of poor mental health. The intensity of school exams, even of the school day itself, leaves young people exhausted and worn out. This pressure comes from a variety of sources – sometimes teachers, sometimes parents, and sometimes from students themselves.

Universities were once the preserve of a very small number of eighteen-year olds. The chance to study something at a higher level, to make sense of the world, to do the kind of very serious and very frivolous things that university students do was the exclusive property of a tiny, wealthy minority. In 1950, just 3.4% of young people went to university.[17] Throughout the last century, universities were opened up to increasingly broad sections of the population. This changed many thousands of people's lives in significant ways. That more and more people have the chance to study, in detail, what they're interested in, with a community of people interested in the same thing is hugely important. The ability to analyse and understand the world should not be the preserve of a rich few. The contemporary university, however, has very little to do with advanced study. This might seem counterintuitive – don't people go to university to study a particular subject? – but degrees are increasingly treated and understood solely as practice for work. Indeed, from students' first day at university, they are reminded of the importance of improving their employability, of the career opportunities that their new

---

17   https://timeshighereducation.com/features/participation-rates-now-we-are-50/2005873.article (last accessed December 2020).

university can bring them. Under conditions like this, learning for its own sake, or for emancipatory, collective ends, becomes impossible.

What happened to the liberatory possibility of higher education, as an opening of horizons? We can trace the source of the rot to changes in the funding regime for higher education in England (education is devolved in Wales, Scotland and Northern Ireland) that took place under the Coalition government of 2010–15. While fees had been introduced by the previous New Labour government, it was under the Tories and the Liberal Democrats that higher education became a market. It is worth saying that these changes are profoundly unfair for individual students, who end up paying back more money the poorer they are. What's mentioned less often, however, is the devastating effect that this has had on universities. Rather than receiving a block grant, the main source of universities' income is now from tuition fees: they receive money per student. The original idea behind this was that it would drive up standards. In fact, the opposite happened. Universities are now in permanent recruit-ment mode, buying whatever gimmicks and massaging whatever statistics are needed to make their courses more appealing than others. The statistics they use to attract students, and those used in mainstream league tables, are figures for things like future job prospects and the number of students getting top degrees. This creates a circular logic: grades are inflated to increase rankings; higher rankings mean more students apply and degrees are looked upon more fondly by employers. This doesn't do anything to actual standards of teaching; it's a bubble.

This bubble is not just pedagogically degrading but misleading and harmful. The figures for the so-called graduate premium are often based on the earnings of graduates from years when far fewer people went to university and before the 2008 global economic downturn. Even ignoring the problems with these figures, the increased earnings amount to about £2,200 per year, which does not even cover the interest accruing on student loan debt.[18] These are also average figures. For many subjects, the figures are lower – medicine compared to history, for example – and men get a bigger wage increase compared to women, white people more than people of colour, and non-disabled people higher than disabled people.

As universities move away from teaching and research and towards student recruitment, they attempt to do more for less, at the cost of working conditions. To keep pace with the fluctuations in student numbers and in funding, universities hire more and more temporary staff. It is much easier and cheaper to both hire and fire temporary staff – you can pay them less and you have fewer duties towards them. Academics have little control over or time to prepare what they teach while working on short-term, temporary contracts. When the actual time it takes for the preparation, teaching, marking and so on, is counted up, lecturers can be paid less than minimum wage.

Students have been sold an impossible dream: work hard, keep studying and you'll be financially rewarded, or at the very least financially secure. After nearly two decades of training in how to become a total entrepreneur, how to maximise your own personality and skills, young people are anxious, miserable and broke. They take on student loans, debt from personal loans or overdrafts, work several part-time jobs, and at the end of it, the promise of a rewarding or less miserable job quickly evaporates. Those young people who have not been to university – the other half of 18 to 21-year-olds – tend to be, partly because of the class character of the journalist class, forgotten. They face,

18 http://if.org.uk/wp-content/uploads/2016/07/Graduate_Premium_final. compressed.pdf (last accessed December 2020).

and without the not insignificant cushioning of graduate status, the same problems of debt, crap jobs and long hours as their degree-holding peers.

The instrumentality of capitalist work spreads over the rest of human social life like a heavy cloud. In the case of education, this instrumentality makes real learning impossible. Genuine learning requires the suspension of instrumentality. It needs a sense of possibility, the possibility of making mistakes, and the possibility of playfulness. It needs reciprocity; it ought to involve learning from each other, a sense of community, and a sense of freedom. These possibilities are nowhere to be found in contemporary education. Instead, school pupils and university students are confronted with a curriculum directed at their future jobs, with immense pressure to succeed, with the odds stacked against them, and most crucially, infused with the most profound kind of instrumentality in which the raw materials to be worked on are one's own personality.

Chapter 6

What does work do to society?

Who built the seven gates of Thebes?
The books are filled with names of kings.
Was it the kings who hauled the craggy blocks of stone?
　　　– Bertolt Brecht, 'Questions from a Worker who Reads'

Work harms us as individuals, eating up our time, leaving us with little left for ourselves or for any other activity outside of work. There is a dark irony in the fact that the classical retirement gift from a firm is a carriage clock. But what about society as a whole? What kind of effects might work under capitalism have on how we collectively live, on how we treat each other, and how our society is structured? Work isn't just something we do for a fixed, albeit growing, number of hours a day. It is one process through which capitalist exploitation takes place and, as such, one of the main institutions through which capitalism is lived. That process produces not only the individual products made in a given workplace, but the world itself – it makes the stuff of everyday life, from the homes we live in, to the technology we use, and the infrastructure that sells and brings it to us – work is world-building. Work is the marshalling of human capacities in all kinds of directions. It's also world-building in a second sense: as well as requiring structural inequality of resources, it draws on and reproduces oppressive norms and power imbalances. It relies on and reinforces a variety of different structural relationships of inequality, in particular, class and ownership, gender and race.

The products of work – whether material or immaterial – make up the world as we experience it. From the perspective of the consumer, this can look like a kind of sorcery. But, as Agnieszka Mróz of Amazon Workers International reminds us, '[w]arehouse workers, not magic, are how freight trucks get unloaded, forklifts get driven, items get picked from endless shelves, and boxes get packed for distribution.'[1] To the consumer, goods appear fully formed, whether they're packed onto supermarket shelves, next day-delivered with Amazon Prime, or clutched by influencers on Instagram. If we think about commodities as objects, we tend to think about how they make us feel (adequate, better, temporarily better, frustrated, cheated) or how they're advertised. Our relationship to our phone, for example, is shaped not by the knowledge of how it was made but by what it might convey about us, and how we might use it in future. The processes, the work, that create the products we buy and that get them to us, is not made visible. This is stark when it comes to modern electronics, which tend to be built not to be tinkered with. We don't know the components that make them up. Repairing objects has become specialist knowledge, hidden to protect profit margins on products with built-in obsolescence. Electronics are not easy to break into fixable components; even the lithium-ion batteries with finite lives cannot be removed and replaced. The electronic guts of laptops are typically soldered together – an early adopter was Apple's 2010 MacBook Air in which the RAM was soldered in, making component upgrading (common at the time) and home repairs much harder.[2] In later models, batteries are glued into the casing, and custom screws are used in order to make it harder to open up the devices.[3]

You need a specially trained eye to see the work that has gone into something. This might be the training that comes from honing a particular skill or craft, knowing how long it would take to make something, the kind of movements and materials required, or it might come from a shift in perspective. Even without the technical know-how of exactly how something was made or brought to the consumer, how much effort it requires, it is possible to reorient our knowledge of the world; to look at a building and wonder who built it, and under which conditions. When we do this, we can see everything around us as a product of human effort, of world-making work.

Shared lives, isolated worlds

The spoils of this world-making work, however, are not equally shared. While capitalism has, so far, been able to produce abundance on a scale that would have been unimaginable before its advent, there is not equal access to this abundance. Moreover, the creation of such abundance deepens inequality as some are able to directly profit from it whereas others are not. Work produces the world, but it is also the process through which the possibilities of a shared lifeworld are eroded. Capitalism is premised on inequality. This equality is not the same kind of inequality that can be found in rigid rank. It often has the shimmer of equality of opportunity, it is justified by claims

2   https://businessinsider.com/why-im-never-buying-an-apple-computer-again-2018-11?r=US&IR=T (last accessed December 2020).
3   https://gizmodo.com/apples-war-on-upgrades-continues-with-the-new-touch-bar-1789002979 (last accessed December 2020).

to meritocracy. But it requires, for it to function, that some people have access to resources that others do not. Especially in societies where it is deepest, this fundamental inequality means that the possibility for shared social lives, and even for mutual comprehension, is massively curtailed. One way to think about this problem is through the philosopher Gerald A. Cohen's idea of the principle of community.

Cohen takes community to require that people care about, and sometimes for, each other.[4] He uses the example of a rich man who, one day, is compelled to take the bus to work. While able to find a feeling of automatic community with his fellow car drivers, he is unable to gripe about his bus-shaped predicament with those who normally take the bus. The two groups – mapping onto inequalities of wealth – lack a shared world, making it harder for them to care for and about each other.[5] The lack of communal feeling felt in Cohen's example also demonstrates the importance of public goods, held in common, built and maintained to a high standard, and intended to be universally used. Having decent public transport systems, or libraries, or sports centres, or hospitals, and making their use easy and, crucially enjoyable or at least pleasant, decreases public support for the establishment of exclusive, private alternatives, ensuring that people have shared lives, as well as providing affordable public services for those who need them.

Cohen's bus example is particularly helpful because it is rooted in the way that relationships of class and power are experienced, are lived. We become so used to these relationships that they often go unremarked on; they become just how things *are*, and sometimes, they appear as if they are how things always

4   Gerald A. Cohen, *Why not Socialism?* (Princeton: Princeton University Press, 2009), p. 34.
5   Ibid., p. 35.

have been and always will be, too. In many ways, the wealthy live entirely separate lives from the population at large, often in gated communities, sometimes with their own security guards. Billionaires have even built their own gated doomsday shelters.[6] Exactly who will work as their future servants, staffing their luxurious bunkers, at the end of the world, isn't clear. But unlike Cohen's bus, where the two, separate life-worlds have only temporarily come into contact, what happens when the two worlds are more firmly attached?

An extreme example can be found in the case of service work done within the employer's home, and the kind of paranoia, resentment, and even outright abuse that it can involve. In 2014, Google's Nest Labs acquired Dropcam, a security camera manufacturer. In the summer of 2015, Google released the Nest Cam, a 1080p interior security camera, with night vision, sound and noise alerts, and a video feed that can be viewed remotely through an app. A later version includes facial recognition.[7] This small camera is not only used for standard home security purposes but is often used to monitor nannies and other workers within homes. While they're not typical in the UK where their covert use is illegal, they are a common practice in the United States, where it's legal to film a care-worker in your home.[8] This is indicative of the broader trend of intrusive, micro-management as technological snooping whereby workers' performance is digitally monitored through software and hardware that their

6 https://edition.cnn.com/style/article/doomsday-luxury-bunkers/index.html (last accessed December 2020).

7 https://bitchmedia.org/article/parents-surveil-nannies-erode-trust (last accessed December 2020).

8 In some states, filming in private spaces like bedrooms and bathrooms is not permitted.

employers own and control.⁹ As well as reflecting deepening technological control, the use of spy cameras like the Google Nest demonstrates the mutual distrust that the unequal relationships of capitalist work cause.

The paranoia that employers feel towards their employees, particularly when the employment involves the kind of emotional intimacy behind closed doors that service and care work in the home require, is palpable. Employers might claim that those they employ are part of the family, but if this is the case then the family is a dysfunctional one. In Bong Joon-ho's 2019 film *Parasite*, the fear inherent in the employer-employee relation comes dramatically to the fore when the Kim family con and bamboozle their way into the wealthy Park family's luxurious home. Posing as different, and unrelated, potential employees – an English tutor, an art therapist, a housekeeper and a chauffeur – the Kims work together to expel the Parks' existing servant employees. The film's dramatic climax starts with the Kims relaxing in the Park home while their employers are on a birthday trip for the youngest Park child, before descending into gory violence. Fêted for its depiction of class conflict and class difference in contemporary capitalism, *Parasite* is as revealing of the psychic contortions of wealth as it is of the Kims' basement-dwelling poverty. In societies, like liberal capitalist democracies, which claim to disavow hierarchy, service work becomes a kind of fearful magic. The wealthy, while benefiting from the inequality that allows them to live well while paying others a pittance, must cope with the fear that comes from being at the top of a hierarchy: the fear not only that this power will be lost, but that it is undeserved, that those 'beneath' you, know enough about you to destroy you.

---

9   See https://common-wealth.co.uk/reports/data-and-the-future-of-work (last accessed December 2020).

The Parks' class anxiety has a similarly dramatic antecedent in Joseph Losey's 1963 film, *The Servant,* where the wealthy Tony hires a new manservant, Barrett. By the end of the film, their roles are reversed, with Tony both terrorised by and dependent – emotionally, practically, and, it is implied, sexually – on Barrett. In both films, the paranoia of the wealthy about their position in societies which disavow unearned hierarchy, a fear intensified by the personal and affective, often intimate work of service work, comes to the fore. That their dominant position might be neither justified nor justifiable causes the wealthy members of society sleepless nights, soothed through their charitable donations and the pretence that they and their employees are really, despite their Google Nests, just one big family. The pretence that employees are part of the family, can make it hard for them to understand and demand their rights as workers; families are supposed to have a shared interest and are supposed to compromise for its sake. Because of the coercive force of the myth of workplace-as-family, workers are unable to demand their rights as workers.

Work, class and status

So far, we have mainly talked in terms of two classes – those who sell hours of their lives, and those who buy that time and profit from it. It's important not to lose sight of this distinction. I have been keen to stress it because this fundamental fact, one that governs our lives and defines our economic system, is so often ignored. However, within this first group – those who must work to live – there is a huge range of experience, gradations that can appear so significant as to call into question the unity of the first group. Those who have to work to live include those with safe, fulfilling, and prestigious jobs, and those eking out pockets of pay, often with no security, and in jobs with little to no prestige, or that are even directly stigmatised. Even the apparent public revaluation of 'essential' jobs or 'key workers' in the wake of Covid-19 tended to talk of doctors and nurses, sometimes NHS staff generally, but very rarely were hospital porters or cleaners included explicitly. Those who worked in social care, despite being twice as likely to die of Covid-19 than the general working-age population,[10] were, by and large, ignored. While the importance of delivery drivers and supermarket shelf-stackers to lockdown living was sometimes mentioned, workers in these less prestigious jobs were rarely offered discounts and public displays of affection.

This oversight might have something to do with the different degrees of esteem placed on different kinds of work. One reason for the social undervaluation of particular work is the associa-tion of that work with women – the fact that it is understood to be women's work. This is the case for elder care, as it is for the care of the very young. This work is typically done by women, partic-ularly by migrant women, and is undervalued partly because of the extreme age-partitioning that characterises contemporary British capitalism, and partly because of the privatisation and deregulation of early years and nurseries as well as of elder care. When a sector or job is associated with women, or 'feminised', it is often poorly paid and not highly valued. Several councils in the UK have faced lawsuits and industrial action over revela-tions that women employed in typically 'female' roles, including dinner ladies, cleaners and home carers, were paid less than com-parable 'male' roles.[11] Gender is one factor, but we can't make

---

10   https://nursingtimes.net/news/coronavirus/covid-19-death-rate-significantly-higher-in-social-care-workers-11-05-2020/ (last accessed December 2020).
11   https://bbc.co.uk/news/uk-england-manchester-16844478 (last accessed December 2020); https://theguardian.com/society/2019/jan/17/glasgow-council-women-workers-win-12-year-equal-pay-battle (last accessed December 2020); https://bbc.co.uk/news/uk-england-birmingham-24383352 (last accessed December 2020).

sense of the social devaluation of certain kinds of work without thinking about the ways in which professional, 'white-collar', 'middle-class' – whatever you want to call them – jobs are valued more highly than in routine and manual work, whether skilled or unskilled, gendered male or female. These two categories – professional and non-professional – can be blurry and contested. Sectors or roles can change in status (whether they're seen as prestigious) as the social value of them is contested (whether people think the work is important, and what 'important' is can change), but the distinction between the two kinds of work – professional and non-professional – remains. Aside from the higher pay for professional occupations, these jobs tend to offer more autonomy and room for self-development, and, crucially, tend to bring recognition and respect from others. The salaries of professional jobs can decline, as has happened across the public sector (apart from at the levels of senior management) where, apart from a small boost in 2020, pay for teachers, ambulance drivers, university staff, nurses and so on, has seen a significant real-terms cut in the past decade.[12] But the status of these jobs has remained even as pay and conditions are eroded. In some cases, these public sector professional jobs can even offer lower average pay than some skilled manual work. Despite this, they still offer recognition and social esteem and social capital, which provides benefits to the individual, and a set of meanings – about fairness, dignity and supporting the public interest among others – that can be used to publicly make the case for improving pay and conditions.

Jobs for the girls

In May 2017, on the campaign trail for re-election, the then Prime Minister, Theresa May, drew harsh criticism after saying

---

12 https://theguardian.com/society/2017/jul/03/damning-government-report-shows-scale-of-public-sector-pay-cuts (last accessed December 2020).

that in her house, there are 'boy's jobs' and 'girl's jobs'. The throwaway remark during a light-touch interview cut through May's self-styling as a feminist: what sort of feminist holds on to outdated notions of gendered domestic tasks? What was interesting about this furore was not the question of whether Theresa May was a feminist or the question of whether she accepted uncritically or refused to challenge received notions of gender (especially as her record of austerity and the hostile environment in government was anything *but* feminist) but that people instinctively knew which jobs might be boys' jobs and which might be girls' jobs. Anything heavy or requiring tools and technologies that aren't used every day would be for the boys, whereas tasks involving mundane technologies, nimble dexterity or those that are primarily a case of reminding and remembering, would be for the girls. Women might order the online shopping, but men would bring it in. The gendered division of labour, whether we like or it not, whether we try to challenge it or not, is one of many received ideas about how people ought to behave. We can think of these practices as a kind of potentially ideological shorthand. They don't just rely on existing ideas about gender but rearticulate them.

Rather than thinking about how a lucky few from oppressed groups can be promoted to the upper echelons of the professional classes, we might consider how low-paid work, often considered 'dirty', typically in poorly paid and poorly socially valued sectors are both a cause and a result of existing relationships of power. When we think about work in these terms, the problem of women's work isn't just a lack of access to certain (prestigious) careers but the problem of the stickiness of particular associations – women as subservient, caring, unskilled; men as strong, skilled and uncaring. Historically, the construction of the categories of skilled and unskilled labour was a central mechanism through which gender was lived and made at work. Of course, some jobs *do* require more skill than others: some tasks require only the generic training that we can expect most people to have obtained through their school and base level of socialisation (this might involve the socialisation of different skills for different genders, too), whereas others require specialist training. However, the exclusion of jobs typically done by women from the legal and social category of skilled work was one method of suppressing women's wages. It helps that the feminine ideal of the loving wife-mother who sacrifices her time to care for others, useful in the first instance for guaranteeing that women take on the bulk of unpaid housework, is able to spill over into paid work too. Caring work is typically either relatively cheap or entirely free. When jobs move from 'male' to 'female', their status and pay can decline, especially after the emergence of the idea of the male wage as 'family wage', covering the household's full costs, which became hegemonic during the nineteenth century.[13]

The construction of skill in relation to gender at work wasn't merely some plot by the bosses; it was supported by male-dominated trade unions that policed the boundaries of skilled work.[14] Similar patterns can be traced for race and ethnicity; with everyday work practices conditioning as well as having as their precondition, ideas about race and ethnicity. The cultural associations, the scripts and shorthand that carry through and reinforce stereotypes about ethnic or racial groups (as thrifty, as lazy, as hardworking or as violent) are drawn on and reshaped through work. When food shopping with her young child, the poet and feminist Audre Lorde heard a young white child, out

---

13 Pat Ayers, 'The Making of Men: Masculinities in Interwar Liverpool', in Margaret Walsh, ed., *Working out Gender* (Ashgate, Aldershot and Brookfield, 1999), p. 67.
14 Joan W. Scott, *Gender and the Politics of History* (New York: Columbia University Press, 1999, eBook).

with her mother, say, while pointing at her child, 'Oh look, mummy, a baby maid'.[15] In the UK, Black women who work as carers or cleaners are less likely to work in private homes than in the public sector, doing the same kind of tasks but in a quite different setting.[16] This doesn't mean that the racial hierarchy this segmentation reveals and maintains is less stark than in the US – where by 1930, three out of five Black women worked as domestic servants[17] – but that its specific articulations are different. There is a very specific violence that even after years of public service, including looking after some of the most vulnerable in society, Caribbean migrants of the Windrush generation (arriving between 1948 and 1973) were denied access to benefits, to healthcare, and even deported. The work of hospital porters, nurses, cleaners and care assistants is vital. It sustains human life, but the low status it affords, related to its position as something that is created by and maintains harmful ideas about race and gender, allows for the cruel treatment of those paid to do it.

Nature's work

We cannot talk about work under capitalism without talking about the planetary damage that capitalism, through work, through human effort, has caused. Some of this is the immense detritus of the modern workplace: the takeaway coffee cups, the printed-out meeting agendas, the branded company workwear, discarded and updated whenever the job is outsourced again.

---

15 Barbara Ehrenreich and Arlie R. Hochschild, *Global Woman: Nannies, Maids, and Sex Workers in the New Economy* (London: Granta, 2003), p. 192.
16 Lucy Delap, *Knowing their Place; Domestic Service in Twentieth-Century Britain* (Oxford: Oxford University Press, 2011), p. 17.
17 Angela Davies, 'The Approaching Obsolescence of Housework', *Women, Race, and Class* (New York: Vintage, eBook), p. 214.

Some is the immense waste and pollution caused by capitalist work, either by work activities or by the preconditions of that work, even in the least polluting workplaces. A system guided by the profit motive above all else is one that is indifferent to environmental degradation so long as profit can be maintained. Climate crisis is already a reality for much of the world; we are beginning to see more frequent droughts, crop failures, and storms, particularly in the countries of the Global South that have done the least to cause the crisis. Even in the relative safety of the UK, extreme weather events – flooding and heatwaves – are becoming more common, and hit the areas with the least resources hardest.

Capitalist work leaves its mark on the landscape. Some of this is obvious and visible (trees cut down, minerals dug out of the ground, roads and railways laid) but some can't always be seen so easily. One such example is antibiotics. Discovered in 1928, penicillin was produced from the 1940s on an industrial scale, using new techniques of American agribusiness. Antibiotics appear only in very small amounts outside of industrial production. Before mass production began, penicillin, the wonder drug that was able to cure Allied troops in huge numbers, was recycled at the front; the urine of soldiers who had been treated with penicillin was collected and recycled.[18] From the early 1940s, it was known that bacteria could become resistant to antibiotics. It was assumed that this was a trait that was inherited vertically, under selective pressures. However, later genetic research has shown that resistance can also be exchanged horizontally, through mobile bits of DNA such as plasmids – extrachromosomal circles of DNA – that are able to 'jump' between conjugating bacteria. Antibiotics have caused huge changes in

---

18   Hannah Landecker 'Antibiotic resistance and the biology of history', *Body & Society*, vol. 22, no. 4, 2016, pp. 19–52, p. 25.

the microbial biosphere, deepening the reservoir of potential forms of resistance that can be passed between bacteria. This can become visible when bacteria attain new forms of resistance rapidly, as was the case with *Acinetobacter baumannii*, a bacterial species that was a benign soil inhabitant, but has become an antibiotic-resistant pathogen. Research has shown that just one horizontal transfer event gave the bacteria 45 resistance genes.[19]

Termed the 'Iraqibacter' because of its prevalence in American military hospitals in Iraq, which spills over into civilian populations in Iraq and in the US, *A. baumannii*, formed in the crucible of sanctions, neo-imperial wars, and other 'interventions' made under the flag of American military capital, is a visible sign of how human effort has had profound effects on the natural world. Hannah Landecker, a historian and sociologist of modern life science, asks us to consider these effects in light of her idea of the 'history of biology', that is, the physical registration of human history in bacterial life. Seen through this conceptual lens, nature isn't a system outside of human life upon which humans act, but something that humans can change in a fundamental way and of which they are dynamically part. Landecker argues that antibiotic resistance is a collective ecological condition of late capitalism, caused by human activity that means that bacteria today are different – physiologically, medically and ecologically – to those that existed before modern antibiotics.

Antibiotics treat infections that previously had a high chance of becoming fatal or life-altering. They've also made surgery, organ transplants and chemotherapy more viable by reducing the likelihood of infection. Childbirth is much less dangerous now too. Despite their obvious importance and the diminishing efficacy of existing variants; no new antibiotics have been

---

19   Ibid., p. 32.

developed since the 1980s. Antibiotics are expensive to make, and crucially, cannot be sold in very large amounts – new antibiotics are supposed to be kept as a drug of last resort – or for high prices. This means that there is little market incentive for antibiotic research and development. At the same time, climate crisis is likely to cause a rise in the number and prevalence of infectious diseases.[20] Work under capitalism cannot meet the deep changes that we need to make to avert climate catastrophe, changes which may or may not alter our standards of living. It is possible that living standards could be maintained or even rise, but it's equally possible, if not more likely, that these could decline. Either way, we can say with certainty that expectations of capitalists – that they will continue to make and invest profits – are not compatible with the continuation of life. Taking them on will require deepening action on multiple fronts: they will not let go of the old, profitable order without a fight. As Andreas Malm, a lecturer in human ecology, warns us, '[t]he ruling classes really will not be talked into action. They are not amenable to persuasion; the louder the sirens wail, the more material they rush to the fire, and so a change in direction will have to be forced upon them.'[21]

I spoke to Adrienne Buller, a Senior Researcher at the think tank, Common Wealth, and a climate activist and writer, about what capitalism means for the environment. She told me:

Fundamentally, finance-dominated capitalist economies have generated staggering inequalities of wealth, and of economic power. It's these inequalities that are driving climate and envi-

20   https://who.int/globalchange/summary/en/index5.html (last accessed December 2020).

21   https://jacobinmag.com/2020/10/ende-gelande-climate-justice-movement-nonviolence (last accessed December 2020).

ronmental catastrophe, and we can't secure a habitable planet without designing a drastically more equal global economy.

Work is a central institution through which capitalism is lived. It is the site and process of value extraction, and this process leaves its mark on the natural world just as much as it does on individual people. Capitalism and work under capitalism have as their precondition and product all kinds of structural inequalities. It has world-transforming capacities because human effort, in all its various forms, has the power to change the world. As it stands, however, these capacities are channelled into activity that causes harm on a massive scale; they are cannibalised, channelled into the destruction of human life.

Chapter 7

Phantoms and slackers: Resistance at work

The SLANTY® toilet has a seat that is angled at between eight and thirteen degrees. This slope means sitting on the toilet quickly becomes uncomfortable; at 13 degrees, it becomes painful to sit on the toilet for more than five to seven minutes.[1] The sloped toilet seat is designed to reduce the amount of time people take in the bathroom. The company behind the toilet is keen to stress its health benefits, claiming that cutting down the amount of time you spend sitting on the toilet is more hygienic and reduces the risk of developing haemorrhoids. This might be the case, although it offers little for the well-being of those with health conditions that mean they are likely to need to spend longer on the toilet. One of the other proposed applications for the SLANTY® is to increase workplace efficiency. They claim that 'an average person spends around 25% greater time in work space [sic] lavatories than necessary', and that by introducing seats that quickly become uncomfortable, employers will increase productivity. This toilet might seem like a controversial outlier, but it's typical of the ways in which management can seek to exert control over workers. It shows us, in vivid and painful detail,

---

1   https://bbc.co.uk/news/technology-50835604 (last accessed December 2020).

a central dynamic in the workplace: that management aims to keep workers busy for the maximum possible time. This control plays out in different ways. Sometimes it is the use of scheduling, sometimes the use of perks like free pizza and beer for those who stay longer into the evening. The use of outright force to ensure people work is no longer common, but it's been replaced by a softer, hidden coercion, like a secretly sloping toilet, reminding you that at work, your time is not your own: it is the company's, and they will try their hardest to keep every second of it.

But what would happen if you refused to play along? What would happen if you just stopped doing your job, and made sure nobody noticed? Such a proposal might feel like the most absurd wish fulfilment or a fever dream, but Joaquin Garcia, a 69-year-old Spanish civil servant, did just this. Despite continuing to draw a salary, Garcia dubbed 'El Funcionario Fantasma' [The Phantom Official] by Spanish newspapers, didn't show up to work for six years. He was eventually fined a year's salary, after tax. Not such a bad deal.[2]

While most of us can only dream of such a feat, many of us do engage in practices of clawing back our time, agency, or thoughts whether at work or against work, or both. Let's start with the most common forms of resistance: individual resistance within the workplace. At one job, I had a colleague who would always make sure to walk the longest possible route around the office, weaving between desks, bumping into colleagues and encouraging small talk that seemed plausibly serious and plausibly work-related to the casual observer. These kinds of practices are very common. One study found that the average office worker spends fifty minutes of their working day avoiding work.[3]

2   https://bbc.co.uk/news/world-europe-35557725 (last accessed December 2020).
3   https://independent.co.uk/life-style/50-ways-of-slacking-off-at-work-a8137436.html (last accessed December 2020).

Of course, not everything we do at work when we should be working is done for pleasure or diversion. The stolen phone call or thumbed phone remind us that the crisis of work is also a crisis of social reproduction; as we are expected to take on more and more paid work, we are simultaneously expected to take on more and more unpaid care work as welfare provisions are cut. But for many, the practices of individual resistance at work are to stave off the boredom that comes from repetitive tasks, and the frustrations that come from the brazen stupidity of the workplace.

A taxonomy of slacking off

The most common practices for resistance at work are probably the small acts of slacking off that allow for an assertion, however limited, of our autonomy. Or at least, our autonomy when we're in the toilet, hiding from our managers and co-workers. Stolen moments where we push back against the managerial proclamations that we find the most outrageous. Tiny skirmishes on a longer-term war over a frontier of control. The first group of these assert a temporary reclamation of our time. Elongating lunch breaks, hanging out with the smokers on their breaks, or even taking up smoking ourselves, spending time on social media and quickly opening a spreadsheet or Word document when a colleague passes behind us, or even applying for other jobs on company time.

These minor acts of time theft can be thrilling or just a tool for getting through the workday. Just as shops expect and plan for lost profits through shoplifting, employers expect a margin of slacking off. These margins are different in different sectors and the extent to which they are permitted depends on the relative power of the workers in that sector, the prestige or expertise that their job is assumed to have, and the technological possibilities for monitoring that work.

In industrialising Britain, factory-owners routinely concealed the time from workers. By turning clocks back and forward, they secretly shortened breaks to maximise profits. Workers knew about this but were able to do little, and those with their own watches could even end up fired.[4] In the contemporary workplace, the battle over time is different. Bosses might not turn back clocks, but in many workplaces, management attempts to cultivate a sense of responsibility and loyalty to the company – one that goes beyond working to contract, encouraging employees to constantly improve their performance. It is not merely enough to be doing the job you were hired to do: you must be improving and developing all the time. Of course, being stuck in the same role forever can be boring, and being denied opportunities for promotion and higher pay can be harmful. But these demands to always be doing better don't usually involve doing better for the sake of promotion down the line but as routine expectation. This means an intensification of work during work hours, with more time taken from employees by a demand for constant improvement which represents an unmeetable, always moving horizon. While workers try to carve out time away from work at work, management intensifies the process of work.

It is against this intensification, and the time theft that it causes, that the second set of workplace resistance practices are targeted. We can broadly group these together as 'strategies for avoiding management', with management referring to managers themselves and the tools and techniques of management, which may or may not be separate from the managers. One strategy is regular working from home. The scope for the monitoring

---

4   E. P. Thompson, 'Time, Work-Discipline, and Industrial Capitalism', *Past & Present*, no. 38, 1967, pp. 56–97, p. 86.

of work by managers is vastly reduced if you're not actually at work. Sometimes, working from home also involves time-grabbing slacking off: one person I know told me that they log in to their remote desktop from bed first thing in the morning, and then go back to sleep for a few hours. Working from home can mean taking longer to do tasks or doing them at different times. While remote monitoring remains largely taboo in the UK, the Covid-19 lockdown saw a rise in interest by companies in the use of software to check workers' activity. This kind of technology often promises a focus on improving team dynamics or employee wellbeing and it is through this softer narrative that it could become normalised.

Another common tactic is to find some way of making yourself indispensable. If you're the only one who knows how something works and that thing is of some importance to the place where you work, there are a couple of ways you can gain a little more control over your daily activity. Sometimes this is minor. If you're a spreadsheet whizz while everyone else at your workplace struggles with working out how to copy and paste text, you can disguise how long it takes to do certain tasks. If nobody else can understand what you do, you can't be monitored and managed as well as someone whose daily tasks are more obvious. If you're a sales assistant in, say, H&M, and that day you're assigned to the denim section, it will quickly become obvious if you have not kept on top of folding each pair of jeans: the jeans will quickly become chaotic, customers won't be able to find the sizes they need, the clothes will start spilling onto the floor. If, by contrast, you're the only person who knows how to batch edit image files, then you can pretend that the task is longer and more strenuous than it really is, asking not to be disturbed in this busy and stressful time. Plus, if the expertise you have is rare and business-essential, the cost of firing you and losing that expertise, with all the possibilities of computer systems crashing, is pretty high. This can give people relative freedom and the ability to say 'no' or delay infuriating demands from their bosses.

While not exactly avoiding management, the next commonly used strategy makes relationships between employers and employees easier. The average person in the UK will change employer every five years.[5] It is likely that young people change jobs more regularly than older people: in the US, the average tenure of workers aged 55 to 64 was 10.1 years, compared to 2.8 years of workers aged 25 to 34.[6]

Many people move quickly between different jobs. While the idea of the universal lifetime job was a myth even during its Fordist heyday, staff turnover is increasing. Turnover is high in low-paid, precarious work. In call centres, the turnover rate is 26% per year, compared to a UK average of 15%. In the care sector, where 24% of jobs are zero-hours contracts, it is 31%.[7] This high level of churn isn't always a concern for employers. In fact, for roles that require only a small amount of training[8] and intense and intensifying patterns of work, a high level of churn might even be desirable for bosses. The Amazon warehouse would be a paradigmatic case. Given the ease of replacing workers and the ability to recuse responsibility for sick, injured or otherwise vulnerable workers in the patchily unionised workforce, a rapid

---

5 www.bbc.co.uk/news/business-38828581 (last accessed December 2020).
6 Ibid.
7 According to Skills for Care, see https://skillsforcare.org.uk/adult-social-care-workforce-data/Workforce-intelligence/documents/State-of-the-adult-social-care-sector/State-of-Report-2019.pdf (last accessed December 2020).
8 These roles are often referred to as 'low skilled', but this category can be misleading. There is certainly a great deal of skill involved in care work or retail work, for example. However, these jobs tend to require very little additional training beyond what is provided in compulsory education or that people generally hold (for example, driving) for most people to start them.

turnover of staff allows for a more fluid intensification of the work process, and an atomised, less unruly workforce.

However, at the level of the individual worker, moving between jobs quickly makes daily working life easier to bear. When a job is new, even a really tedious one, there are a few exciting diversions: getting to know colleagues, getting to know the tasks you are expected to do, pushing at the limits of management's expectations (what can you get away with and what can you not get away with), what kinds of places you can go to for lunch, what kind of coffee machine your workplace has, what the light is like at dusk in a particular part of the building. While these might seem trivial in the brute face of exploitation and widespread misery, these form an important part of the daily experience of work. Against the relentless misery and intensification of low-paid work, novelty can be better than familiarity. Novelty breaks up monotony, at least for a while.

Perhaps the most basic and common forms of resistance in the workplace are those that take place just within the mind of an individual worker. That workplaces make demands on sociability is nothing new. Seventy years ago, American sociologist, C. Wright Mills, identified a phenomenon that he termed the 'personality market': office workers were increasingly expected to use and develop elements of their personality for and within their careers. These demands are now commonplace – even, and often especially, in poorly paid work. Refusing to understand your personality as grist for the mill, as something to be developed in the service of your employer, or complying only outwardly with the demands placed on you is common. Refusing to love your job, refusing to see it as the most important thing in your life can become a form of resistance when your employers (specific or in general) demand that you emotionally bind yourself to your work. Sometimes the refusal of the affective demands of work spills over into the refusal of particular tasks. More often, it remains at the level of refusing to seriously engage with the most frustrating demands of the workplace.

You can, of course, leave your job. In some ways, this can be leveraged as a threat: if you make me do something I don't want to do, I'll just leave. Such threats only work well when you're hard or expensive to replace. This isn't the case for most workers, particularly in times of high unemployment and low unionisation. For most workers, you need your job much more than your job needs you.

Workers, Monitored

The 2001 UK TV series, *The Office*, is a searing critique of the interpersonal inanity of work. You are stuck with appalling people, day in and day out, usually doing something that means very little to you subjectively and contributes even less to society as a whole. What's worse is that you are expected to bring yourself to care about it. This frustration bubbles over into squabbling and skiving. In a memorable scene, one character encases a co-worker's special stapler in jelly. Their boss, showing around a new employee, explains that 'it's mad here'. Office work becomes an empty parody of real human social life. A dried-up husk of having to pretend to laugh, having to pretend to care, engage in small talk and business talk indefinitely. Futures postponed; emails answered.

While *The Office* tapped into widespread feelings of resentment and boredom, typical office workers actually represent something of a privileged group when it comes to the ability to resist the most egregious parts of work. Most of the examples of possible resistance listed so far rely on having a relative degree of autonomy over your work. In a modern office, many workers will be responsible for a variety of different tasks (taking minutes, making phone calls, writing briefings, sending emails, calculating budgets, and so on), that would have previously been done by people with specialised skills (typists, telephonists, copyists, and so on). While outputs are monitored periodically, or when something goes catastrophically wrong, the day-to-day work process, is, to some extent, within the control of the individual worker.

While it is possible for the activity of office workers to be monitored, the routine use of monitoring is frowned upon. Office workers know the processes by which they are assigned work and know how to use the software they must use to carry it out. This makes these practices of skiving much easier. By contrast, many workers do not have any control over how, when and where they do particular tasks at work. In his study of Deliveroo riders, Callum Cant describes the experience of being managed by opaque algorithmic technology, through an app:

> Speculation about how the app worked was rife. Elaborate theories were developed . . . One popular one was that our location was scanned every five seconds, and the person closest to the restaurant during the five-second when the restaurant calls the rider gets the order. But these theories were a combination of guesswork and rumour . . . The knowledge of how our work was coordinated was hidden from us.[9]

When the output of your work is measured, and your every movement is mapped, failing to meet the expected standards can cause you significant problems. The technology of the modern workplace is not the neutral driver of efficiency of Silicon Valley

---

9 Cant, *Riding for Deliveroo*, p. 59.

legend, but something coercive, towering over workers, acting as an extension of management's power over them. The disciplinary powers of technology don't stop the practices of slacking off outlined above – people have always found ways to claw back their time – but they do make them harder. If conditions for workers in formerly prestigious professional work deteriorate, we are likely to see these coercive monitoring practices becoming more generalised. Your boss doesn't need to watch over your shoulder if your computer monitors how long you spend on each task.

To get a sense of what this kind of monitoring is like, we should consider an example that is at once the most advanced and the most banal case of a technologically managed workplace: the call centre. The theorist Mark Fisher argued that call centre workers, what he termed 'banal cyborgs', were the paradigmatic contemporary worker. For the estimated 1 million call centre workers in 5,000 UK call centres, the frontier of control between workers and managers is felt continuously.[10] For call centre workers, the possibility of a call being pulled up and getting you into trouble is a very real one. Every encounter with a customer could feasibly be recalled at any moment.[11]

I spoke to Morgan Powell, a former call centre worker, and sociology researcher, about control and resistance in call centres:

I worked in three call centres over two years. Each one fostered the same sense of powerlessness. The pace of the working day was set by automated call queues and strict targets. The initial nervousness of starting the job quickly turned into boredom when the hundreds of calls blurred into one another, with most people repeating the same mundane problems over

---

10   Jamie Woodcock, *Working the Phones* (London: Pluto Press, 2016), p. 21.
11   Ibid., p. 7.

and over. This monotony was only ever punctured by abusive calls, which could throw you off balance for weeks. Racist and sexist abuse was rife and hanging up on such customers was considered a sackable offence and strictly monitored through constant computerised surveillance.

The camaraderie among workers was all that made it bearable – the sense that we had each other's backs. More experienced workers would quietly share advice with new recruits on which managers to avoid, how to get away with things like faking illness, and how to manipulate the call systems. The same technology that enabled surveillance also opened opportunities for resistance. People found and shared ways of cheating or overloading the call queue, forcing computers to crash, even hanging up on abusive callers by 'failing' to transfer them properly.

This kind of informal resistance was never enough to fundamentally challenge management, but it gave us glimpses of power at work and made important differences to our collective working lives.

What are we resisting?

What should we make of the widespread practices of slacking off? The response from managers and management theorists is normally that people should use their time more efficiently, and that this slacking off happens because diligent workers aren't given enough to excite them, and lazy workers, are, well, lazy. I don't find this to be a very satisfying explanation for a widespread disenchantment in workplaces. Work is unable to hold people's attention; it does not provide them with the meaning that they had been promised it would have.

It's easy to see why some have taken the generalised boredom and minor acts of corporate sabotage outlined above as proof of a widely felt resistance to work. There is a great amount of informal resistance that happens within workplaces. But there is, to my mind, a question remaining. What exactly do these practices of resistance resist? In many cases, people still hold out hope (wrongly or rightly) that their next job will be better, will finally offer them meaning and recognition, a nice boss, a better salary and so on. Anger, routine humiliation, feelings of exploitation, and the practices of resistance that function as their pressure valves often have as their targets elements of their current job (an annoying task or a crap manager) rather than the whole edifice of work.

This doesn't mean that there's nothing to this widespread resentment. The promise of work, expressed in our individual jobs, is beginning to appear more illusory to more and more people. Rather than making us rich and happy, work leaves most of us poor and miserable.

How do we gain control? Acting as individuals doesn't get us very far, even if it does mean we can cope with the worst bits of our jobs. That there are so many acts of minor sabotage, individual and largely uncoordinated, point instead to the urgent need to politicise frustrations at work or with work. One way to do so is the subject of the next chapter: building workers' power through trade unions.

I want to return to the story of the Phantom Official. You can hide at work, turn yourself into a ghost if your workplace isn't totally monitored. The Phantom Official became something of a folkloric figure. In a similar way to the folk hero status of bandits or pirates, he offered us the fulfilment of our (more banal) wishes: life and pay without the boss's breath down our necks.

If you're in a sector and a workplace with a high level of trade union membership, your metamorphosis is better guaranteed.

If, however, you work in a sector where employers have the upper hand – say, for example, one in which joining a union is likely to get you blacklisted[12] – things are much more difficult. In 2019, one construction worker enacted the fantasies of revenge many of us have had about our workplaces. When his employers didn't pay him for his work, he destroyed the front of the newly built Travelodge he had been working on. He was jailed for five years and four months.

While the case of the damaged Travelodge is an extreme one, it points to something important. Most people have so little control over their work, and workers have so little power within society, that when faced with a problem at work (unpaid wages, a cruel boss, racist or sexist harassment) there is very little we can do. While we can dream of Phantom Officials and nibble out time for ourselves in our work, without mass coordination of our frustrations, without social transformation, the best we can hope for is that our next job might be slightly less bad.

---

12   https://tribunemag.co.uk/2019/05/blacklisting-a-british-tradition (last accessed December 2020).

Chapter 8

Getting together: Organised labour and the workers' dream

So you tell me that your last good dollar is gone, And you say that your pockets are bare, And you tell me that your clothes are tattered and torn, And nobody seems to care, Now don't tell me your troubles, No, I don't have the time to spare, But if you want to get together and fight, Good buddy that's what I want to hear – Phil Ochs, 'That's What I Want to Hear'

Eight thousand workers gather in the Cimetière de la Chartreuse in Bordeaux. It is October 1848 and the left has just suffered a painful defeat. The crowd is celebrating someone lost a few years before the ill-fated uprising of 1848. The workers have clubbed together to buy a white column inscribed with 'To the Memory of Madame Flora Tristan, author of *The Workers' Union*. The Grateful Workers. Liberty, Equality, Fraternity'. Atop the column is a stone version of her 1843 book *The Workers' Union*.

Tristan is a perplexing figure, a self-styled pariah, usually only mentioned in history books to lament that she's not nearly remembered enough, but she was the first person to imagine an international organisation of workers, doing so five years before the publication of Marx and Engels' *Communist Manifesto*. In fact in 1843, Marx and Engels had barely met. After the publication of *The Workers' Union*, Tristan began a tour that aimed not to merely publicise the book but to bring into existence the ideas at the heart of it. Tristan argued for the formation of an international association of workers, including a paid 'Defender' who would be selected by the workers. The union, funded by small subscriptions paid by members, would secure recognition of the right to work and protest against encroachments on the rights, freedom, and autonomy of workers. It would build Palaces for Workers, where children would be educated (both technical and intellectual training), where the sick would be treated, and the old and disabled cared for. These would be centres not just of work and training but of working-class culture, not only improving the individual lot of workers but for building their power and collective might.

She travelled across France, held mass meetings, raising money, visiting factories and workers' political clubs. Police searched her lodgings and some of the meetings of her tour were banned.[1] Several towns set up branches of her organisation, but the tour took a toll on Tristan's health. By the time she reached Bordeaux in September 1844, she was extremely weak, dying not long after, possibly of typhoid fever.[2] The workers from the union branches she had founded clubbed together to pay for the monument that would be placed on her grave four years later.

Before Tristan, associations of workers existed; these, however, tended to belong to specific trades and places. Efforts had begun to coordinate the welcoming of workers moving

---

1 Marie M. Collins, Sylvie Weil-Sayre 'Flora Tristan: Forgotten Feminist and Socialist', *Nineteenth-Century French Studies*, Summer 1973, vol. 1, no. 4, Summer 1973, pp. 229–34, p. 233.

2 G. D. H Cole, *Socialist Thought, the Forerunners* (London, Macmillan & Co, 1953), p. 186.

between towns and associations, but her proposal was the first to unite all workers – she took this to mean all those who worked with their hands – into one organisation. Tristan wanted national and international coordination of workers. Combined together, she thought, they would be much more powerful than they were as separated individuals or competitive trade bodies.

Flora Tristan had visited London in the 1830s. There, she had attended a host of radical meetings. She snuck into Parliament, where she saw the Irish MP Daniel O'Connell speak. O'Connell received lots of small donations or subscriptions from a large number of ordinary people. From this Tristan developed her idea of paying for a 'People's Defender' from the subscriptions to her workers' union. As Tristan noted in the essays she published on her visits, England, and London in particular, were the grubby core of the newly industrialising and intensely unequal economy.

Another foreign visitor to England, a decade later and similarly shocked by the heinous conditions of emergent industrial capitalism, was Fredrich Engels. The material he collected and research he undertook during this period would form the backbone of one of the earlier texts he would write with Marx, *The Communist Manifesto*. In response to the early struggles of the labour movement, they wrote: 'Now and then the workers are victorious, but only for a time. The real fruit of their battles lies, not in the immediate result, but in the ever-expanding union of the workers.'[3]

Strength in numbers

Workers are numerically the largest class in society, but as individuals, are isolated and atomised. Bringing them together, the

---

3   Karl Marx & Frederich Engels, *The Communist Manifesto* (London: Penguin, 2002), p. 229.

theory goes, in political combination, in a union, makes them more powerful than they would be alone. Unions have two goals which at times overlap, but at other times are in conflict with each other. The first of these is the immediate betterment of conditions in a given workplace. This might be increasing wages or improving conditions – from break room facilities to parental leave. Such demands respond to events like the introduction of a new contract or the firing of colleagues. The second goal is the kind emphasised by Marx and Engels in the quote above: the 'ever expanding union', the bringing of more and more workers into unions, the increasing of their political consciousness and the building of their collective power. This goal relies on a high proportion of the population being members of a union. The same goal relies on a high proportion of a workforce in a site or sector being members of a union. The ambition of this second goal varies: in some cases, it is the winning of greater power and political representation for the working class in a region, sometimes in a country, and sometimes globally.

For as long as there have been trade unions, there have been attempts to restrict them, often involving violence, imprisonment, and legal restrictions on workers' ability to join together. In their early years, workers' organisations tended to be secretive. This clandestinity receded as unions became officially recognised and legally protected organisations during the 1820s.[4] After decades of intermittent victory and repression, trade unions gained the right to strike, to picket, protection for their funds and protection against legal action for breach of contract by employers.

Trade unions have won all kinds of legal protections and benefits for workers – sick pay, paid annual leave, limits on

---

4   Henry Pelling, *A History of British Trade Unionism* (Houndsmill, Basingstoke, Hampshire & New York, Palgrave Macmillan, 1992), p. 23.

the maximum working day, paid parental leave, fighting unfair dismissal and breach of contract, even the right to time off each weekend. But these victories remain fragile, with relentless attacks on trade unions' ability to organise, seemingly without abatement, and with increasing speed under neoliberalism. A raft of anti-union legislation, limiting the right to strike, criminalising some forms of picketing, and making secondary action – action taken to support workers in a different workplace, a formal form of solidarity – was brought in during the 1980s by the Conservatives. When Labour regained power in 1997 this legislation was not undone. To make matters worse, a new Trade Union Act in 2016 placed further restrictions on union activity, making it harder to conduct ballots of members for industrial action and limiting the political activity of trade unions. Together, this means that the UK has some of the worst anti-union legislation in Europe.

These attacks on hard-won legal rights have been justified by an ideological sleight of hand that positions unions and their members as greedy. The establishment likes to paint trade union members as alternately gullible – led by selfish leaders into pointless disputes – or greedy, asking for something they don't deserve. University staff raised concerns about returning to in-person working in the autumn of 2020, worried (and rightly so, it transpired) about a second wave of Covid-19. These were raised in Parliament by Richard Burgon, the Labour MP for Leeds East. When Burgon pointed out that the scientific advice suggested that in-person work was dangerous, the Education Secretary, Gavin Williamson, replied that concerns about health and safety were just those of the University and College Union, on whose behalf Burgon was talking. Implicit in Williamson's response is the idea that unions do not and cannot act in the universal interest, and that employers and government do; unions are partial and selfish, whereas employers act in the interest of everyone. A cursory glance at history, or, hopefully, the pages of this book, will show that this is not the case. Employers do not act in the interests of everyone. In this case, universities were desperate to reopen campuses early to guarantee student fees and rent as revenue. Employers are not guided by a benevolent universal humanism, but by the profit motive. If anything, trade unions, while just as partial as employers insofar as they act in the interest of their members, are more likely to benefit society as a whole. Even while individual actions may temporarily disadvantage non-members, the victories they win and the power for ordinary people that they develop can spill over into other struggles, too. Despite this, the ideological myth of the greedy unions looking for more than they 'deserve' is a mainstay of the establishment press, remaining so even as the actual power of unions has declined.

From defence to hope

With the dismantling of Britain's industry at the end of the last century came a loss of union density – the service sector that replaced industry tends to have fewer union members and tends not to be covered by recognition agreements that allow unions to represent and negotiate for their members.[5] The number of members in the public sector tends to be higher but cuts to the number of jobs available in the public sector, as well as persistent outsourcing and agency work, have squeezed public sector union density, too. In 1979, there were 13 million members of trade

---

5   https://assets.publishing.service.gov.uk/government/uploads/system/uploads/attachment_data/file/887740/Trade-union-membership-2019-statistical-bulletin.pdf (last accessed December 2020).

unions in the UK.[6] In 2019, there were only 6.44 million,[7] 23.5% of workers.[8] Trade union members tend to be older than the average worker: over three quarters of union members were aged over 35 in 2019, compared to 63% of employees in that year. And while recent years have seen a mini surge in union membership, with 100,000 people joining a union in 2017/18 alone,[9] overall membership is still nowhere near its peak.

These relentless attacks have pushed unions into a defensive position, protecting the workplaces that are relatively well organised and which do have recognition agreements. This strategy, if we can call it that, does have a certain sense to it. If you've not got much of something left, it seems intuitive to focus on maintaining what you have, rather than trying to win more. But it can become akin to protecting the few remaining sandcastles on a beach where the tide is rapidly coming in. The same is true in individual workplaces, in those sandcastles; rather than making new gains, historic victories are propped up against always-encroaching erosion. As we saw in Chapter 3, the bogus self-employment typical of the modern gig economy, along with outsourcing, which pits workers against each other, allow employers to duck the costs and responsibilities they would have for direct employees. This makes the challenges unions face even greater.

---

6   Len McCluskey, *Why you should be a trade unionist* (London and New York: Verso, 2019), p. 6.

7   https://assets.publishing.service.gov.uk/government/uploads/system/uploads/attachment_data/file/887740/Trade-union-membership-2019-statistical-bulletin.pdf (last accessed December 2020).

8   https://assets.publishing.service.gov.uk/government/uploads/system/uploads/attachment_data/file/887740/Trade-union-membership-2019-statistical-bulletin.pdf (last accessed December 2020).

9   https://tuc.org.uk/blogs/trade-union-membership-rises-100000-single-year-challenges-remain (last accessed December 2020).

It's easy to slip into despair, to imagine this decline as terminal. But the trade union movement has faced and fought off the legal and political restrictions it's up against now many times before. It's been up against violence, even deadly violence, and the black-listing of workers – effectively enforced penury. There are some green shoots of hope too. Firstly, in the wake of Covid-19, many more people joined trade unions. In my union, the University and College Union (UCU), membership grew by 8,000 between November 2019 and November 2020, compared to 1,000 new members the preceding year.[10] During the first lockdown of 2020, over 20,000 teachers and education workers joined the NEU.[11] Legal attacks on trade unionism have had unintended positive consequences in that the high threshold required for ballots for industrial action (while, of course, unfair and unjusti-fiable) have forced unions to more deeply organise workplaces, with the possibility of making action bigger and more powerful. While extraordinarily repressive, in some cases, this rule also functioned as something of a kick up the arse for unions that had retreated into their defensive comfort zone, focusing on offering individual support and benefits to members, rather than developing members as collective political agents.

The way out of the malaise isn't easy. It's a long, arduous and often frustrating process – hard, unglamorous work over a long time. But, ideally, reaching the point where unions are able to scale up and coordinate individual resistance to despotism at work, and to translate specific gripes about individual workplaces into a universal political programme. Flora Tristan had this ambition, but so do modern union organisers. For

---

10   https://twitter.com/ucu/status/1324746790613241856 (last accessed December 2020).

11   https://ft.com/content/4613a279-e2ac-40f0-a515-0350003b9e31 (last accessed December 2020).

instance, the American organiser and theorist of social change, Jane McAlevey, has argued for a set of tactics that have significant crossover with Tristan's programme. Both stress the importance of building a wide base rather than merely encouraging the already committed to come out in support of something, and, crucially, on considering the lives of workers in the round – in their homes, communities and places of worship as well in their workplace. They both recognise that people don't just stop being workers when they clock out, that being disempowered stretches across your sleeping and waking hours, and conditions your experiences. Both argue for struggle in the terrain of social reproduction as well as more typical bread-and-butter workplace issues. They do so for different reasons and in response to different contexts: Tristan is responding to the intense dislocations and extreme poverty that characterised industrial capitalism, and McAlevey to the increasing dominance of service work and the kinds of shared political struggle (between, say, teachers and parents) that this could afford.

McAlevey argues that rather than shallow mobilising, trade unions need to deeply organise, inspiring workers to 'radically change their lives in all aspects'.[12] This means moving away from a defensive strategy of protecting and policing the movement's deteriorating and fragile gains and towards workplaces that haven't yet been organised. Whether in newly organised sectors or those which have a longer history of union activity, McAlevey extends this strategy of mass participation to include more of the workforce in union negotiations. This is tactically important as well as modelling the kinds of expansive democratic relationships that the workers' movement ought to be run on. It might also be considered a reparatory approach, attempting to acknowledge and address historical harms that have taken place

---

12   Jane McAlevey, *No Shortcuts* (Oxford: Oxford University Press, 2016) p. 66.

when the union movement has ignored or even betrayed rank-and-file members. One sore betrayal can be found in the legal and social category of skilled work and the broader relationship between unions and gender. Male-dominated unions excluded women from their membership and in collective agreements, and conspired with employers to keep women's pay low and their work categorised as 'unskilled'. To take just one sector and one industrial action, in February 1970, in Leeds, women clothing workers in factories across the city walked out of their workplace in an unofficial strike over pay. The strike lasted a month, and at its high point, some 20,000 workers were on strike. Despite the scale of the strike and its innovation in tactics – women workers went from workplace to workplace encouraging workers to walk out, known as 'flying pickets' – the male-dominated National Union of Tailors and Garment Workers refused to lend their support, and instead encouraged the women to go back to work.[13] The strike was partly a response to an agreement between the NUTGW and the employers the previous year which entrenched low wages, primarily for women, and the sector's first ever national productivity agreement. Despite the obvious strength of feeling of the women workers, the NUTGW issued a statement claiming that '[I]t is a negation of everything the trade union movement stands for to break an agreement so obviously beneficial to the vast majority of the membership'.[14]

In response to the male control of unions, some feminists argued that women should not join trade unions – that they were irreparably bad.[15] While the legacy of sexist protectionism,

---

13   Liz Leciester, 'The 1970 Leeds' clothing workers' strike: representations and refractions', *Scottish Labour History Society Journal*, 44, 2009, pp. 40–55, pp. 41–2.
14   Ibid.
15   For example, Selma James 'Women, the Unions and Work, Or, What Is Not To Be Done', *Radical America*, vol. 7, no. 4–5, 1973.

particularly over 'skill' might make these attitudes under-standable, this is completely the wrong approach; unions are institutions that need to be struggled within as well as through. Unions are representative bodies of the working class, but they are not representative mechanically, automatically, but rather through political struggle and political contestation. At the moment, they hover, as Flora Tristan did, somewhere separate to and above workers. Tristan navigated this tension through the use of what we might term the feminine messianic; a self-fash-ioning as a morally and culturally cleansing figure. By contrast, McAlevey argues for a slow, dedicated intervention, a growing tide of ordinary people who join together, looking towards and working for a collective horizon of a better life for all.

When we snap

As with other political movements, work can have a 'snap' – a moment when we feel we simply can't take it anymore: a demeaning request from a manager, petty recrimination for minor infractions like lateness, a sudden awareness that your hard work profits the firm but brings little benefit to you. A moment, in short, in which the connections between our individual experience and underlying structures, the power relations of society, become obvious and clear. The cultural theorist, Sara Ahmed talks about a 'feminist snap', a sudden movement, an optimistic motion, cutting through bonds that harm, and towards new, feminist relations. We can imagine that there is a similar motion when it comes to work, to class consciousness. Unlike feminism, where today there is often no obvious political organisation through which such a snap can be made sense of – the contemporary feminist often snaps alone, finding refuge in reading – at work, the snap should be lived through trade unions, which should be able to translate a gripe into a political concern and eventually into collective action. With the union coordinating action, the snap becomes a wager: workers enter into something political, something collective, something dangerous in the short term that could change the course not just of their own lives, but of collective life. A set of organisations that transform politics, turning it from something that is done to working people to something that ordinary people do themselves.

Trade unions have been and will be vitally important to winning and protecting gains for workers and for building working-class power. There are, however, two limits on the scope of their activity that it is important to note. The first of these is that they involve *workers*. Work is a dominant feature of capitalism and a central institution through which profit is generated and through which people experience capitalism, rubbing up against its contradictions and relations. However, there is a great deal of exploitation that takes place under capitalism that is not to do with work. Chief among these is the exploitation of those who cannot afford to buy their own property by landlords. Besides extra-work exploitation, there are many people who are outside of work, who are not employed. In the latter case, unions have tried to bring the unemployed into their organising fold, for example with Unite's Community initiative, or the National Unemployed Workers Movement in the 1920s, and [benefits] Claimants Unions in the 60s and 70s. As unemployment grows, this kind of activity will become all the more important. Similarly, trade unions should work with and support community organising initiatives, like ACORN or tenants' unions.

I spoke to Rohan Kon, an organiser with Sheffield Needs a Pay Rise and a member of ACORN about the importance of building working-class power within and beyond workplaces:

Organising, wherever it takes place, is the process of building leadership to win tangible change through collective action. Where we draw false distinctions between the workplace and wider community, we artificially compartmentalise our lives and limit our organising solutions to issues, from pay and hours to housing and public services.

Creating a community of low wage workers, fighting alongside our families, friends and neighbours, is a powerful force to win huge gains for the working class. Fresh models of organising, pioneered by ACORN and Sheffield Needs A Pay Rise, offer hope in our mission to unionise the next generation of exploited workers.

The second limitation on the scope of trade union activity is related to the one that ACORN and other organisations are attempting to address through deep organising. This is that most trade union activity in the UK has never risen above the level that Lenin termed 'trade union consciousness', the belief in the importance of combination, of fighting employers and passing legislation. Most of today's unions might not even meet that threshold, instead focusing on defending victories in a small number of workplaces. The boundary of such an approach is the perimeters of each workplace. Even at what was retrospectively one of the high-water marks of British trade unionism, the sociologist Huw Beynon could worry that the workers he observed in the Ford plant in Liverpool being unable to get beyond what he termed a 'factory class consciousness' which 'understands class relationships in terms of their direct manifestation in conflict between the bosses and the workers within the factory', a conflict over control of the job and of conflicting 'rights' of managers and employers.[16] It can't resolve the problem

16   Huw Beynon, *Working for Ford*, p. 98.

of conflict, however, because 'trade union activity in itself is manifestly incapable of altering the entire raison d'être of the capitalist enterprise.'[17]

None of this means that the struggles trade union activists engage in within individual workplaces are not significant. Anyone who has had the experience of working in a sector with significant union density and activity will be able to tell you the difference that makes in comparison to how quickly the bottom can fall out of work in sectors with fewer protections. However, the limits of this trade union or factory consciousness put a ceiling on their ability to reduce the harms of work, particularly in that they are structurally unable to transform rather than improve work. Workers do not have much power in their workplaces. Even when combined in a trade union their collective power remains, usually, quite limited in its scope. They might have the power to prevent practices that are out of step with the contracts and agreements made between the union and the employers. While this could mean protection against unfair dismissal or regulations on overtime, it doesn't mean that workers can make decisions about the day-to-day running of their workplaces. The running of workplaces, for the most part, is in the hands of managers, or in the automated processes, gadgets or robots that are partially usurping them. This division of labour between those who actually carry out the tasks and those who measure and enforce them is a source of all kinds of frustration and mutual distrust.

To see how the self-organising of workers has led to the transformation of work, we should turn to two partially fulfilled dreams of a better world. In these two experiments in worker control, it is not just winning better pay or conditions, but ownership and even the division of labour that are called into

---

17   Ibid., p. 104.

question. The first of these experiments in workers' control was the Paris Commune of spring 1871. The Commune was a worker-led insurrection that lasted for 72 days.[18] It took its aim at not just production but all of social life. Its participants were largely working-class Parisians who, in the words of academic Kristin Ross, had spent most of their time 'not working but *looking for work*'.[19] They reimagined education, combining intellectual and technical learning, developing young minds in a holistic way.[20] The intention here, as was their approach when it came to production proper, was to do away with a hierarchical division of labour. As the Women's Union for the Defense of Paris and Aid to the Wounded put it, '[w]e want power, but in order to keep the product. No more exploiters, no more masters.'[21] This attitude was carried into the workplace. One of the first actions of the Commune was to abolish hated night work for bakers along with child labour. Workers were given the power to take over and run firms themselves and employers were banned from levying fines against workers.[22] The balance of power had shifted decisively in favour of ordinary people, united in changing their own lives for and by themselves. This had a transformative effect, with the emancipation of labour, as Marx would put it in his history of the uprising, meaning that 'every man becomes a working man and productive labour ceases to be a class attribute.'[23] This radical reimagining of human life was, perhaps unsurprisingly, put down, violently and repressively; the French state recaptured the city in 1871, murdering thousands of communards in the process, and scattering survivors across Europe. The Paris Commune

---

18   Kristin Ross, *Communal Luxury*, (London & New York: Verso, 2016), p. 1.
19   Ibid., p.3.
20   Ibid., p. 43.
21   Ibid., p. 28.
22   Karl Marx, *Civil War in France* (Peking: Foreign Languages Press, 1970), p. 78.
23   Ibid., p. 72.

changed the lives of many of its participants fundamentally, and still acts as a beacon, showing what could be, to this day.

The second experiment in worker control is one that didn't even get a chance to be put down or betrayed because it was not permitted to come into existence. This was the Lucas Plan: a concrete dream of reimagined production, preserving jobs and producing socially useful products. It was a response to the threat of a firm's closure – in this case, Lucas Industries, a UK company involved in military production – and to management's predictable response to economic crisis – as the slogan goes: cuts, job losses, money for the bosses. The plan was drawn up between 1975 and 1976, drawing on and developing the tacit knowledge of the production process that workers possess. A questionnaire was sent to all union members, asking them what they thought they should be making. Through this, 150 ideas for products made using existing machinery and with workers' existing skill sets were dreamt up. These included kidney machines and portable life support machines, along with other medical devices; alternative energy sources such as technology for solar and wind power, along with the more outlandish, like a road-rail vehicle, able to avail itself of the road and the railway network.[24]

The plan was published in January 1976 and was praised from many corners, even in that bastion of the liberal status quo, the *Financial Times*. It was nominated for a Nobel peace prize in 1979.[25] Management, however, didn't take it seriously. It didn't help that one of its early supporters, the then Secretary of State for Industry, Tony Benn, was no longer in post. Without support from Westminster and with management hellbent on their plans for closure, the trade unionists found themselves isolated, and

---

24   https://redpepper.org.uk/a-real-green-deal/ (last accessed December 2020).
25   https://theguardian.com/science/political-science/2014/jan/22/remembering-the-lucas-plan-what-can-it-tell-us-about-democratising-technology-today (last accessed December 2020).

their democratic and green vision shelved. This kind of transformative vision, making use of the tacit knowledge of workers, offers the possibility of reorienting production away from arms and environmental degradation and towards socially valuable, life-sustaining productive activity.

The Paris Commune and the Lucas Plan remind us that the development of political representation for the working class, in workplaces, in sectors, in countries, and internationally is not merely to make the case for better rights in some idealised marketplace of ideas, but rather to turn the entire world on its head. Developing power is about winning power, with the goal not merely being heard, of making the case, but of *winning* power to transform the world, not to merely tinker round its edges. From Flora Tristan to the spirit that inspires recent trade union victories – from council workers in West Dunbartonshire saving reserved time for union activists, to the RMT winning the real living wage for almost all railway (train and premises) workers and cleaners, from saving pay and conditions and reducing working hours at Cammell Laird shipyard in Merseyside, to mass action in Bexley, London by bin workers, and by private hire drivers in London, and by care workers in Birmingham, and in Haringey, with the latter case establishing that time workers spend travelling between appointments should count as working time, a significant legal victory[26] – this fragile hope for an ever expanding union, not just for 'better' work but

---

26   https://morningstaronline.co.uk/article/west-dunbartonshire-reps-hit-back-against-snp-councils-attacks-facility-time (last accessed December 2020); https://rmt.org.uk/news/rmt-secures-massive-low-pay-victory/ (last accessed December 2020); https://bbc.co.uk/news/uk-england-merseyside-42690268 (last accessed December 2020); https://tribunemag.co.uk/2020/08/how-the-bexley-bin-workers-won (last accessed December 2020); https://iwgb.org.uk/post/5c4f26006ea6a/biggest-ever-minicab-protest-a; https://magazine.unison.org.uk/2020/09/29/the-best-of-trade-union-empowerment-the-story-behind-a-decisive-homecare-legal-victory/ (last accessed December 2020).

for a better world, has animated workers for centuries. It has been and remains a shared horizon, surpassing the limits of the shop floor. Climate crisis means that this vision – of workplace democracy, and of the transformation of work – is more urgent than ever. We face an existential threat to planetary life; recapturing the spirit of the Lucas Plan, bringing in its principles of socially valuable, environmentally friendly production, that not only protects but democratises work, must play an important part in the struggle that lies ahead.

Chapter 9

Time off: Resistance to work

'I'm not making a career move', I started to explain, but I went no further. 'I'm taking some time off. I'm going to sleep for a year.' – Otessa Moshfegh[1]

'For Mother's Day I asked for one thing: a house cleaning service.' – Gemma Hartley[2]

Capitalism means that most people have to work. It's perhaps not surprising, then, that the most famous examples of those who simply refused to work are literary ones. Chief among these, and a progenitor of a slogan of the post-work movement, is Herman Melville's Bartleby. In Melville's short story, originally published in 1853, the eponymous legal clerk, initially a diligent employee, responds to requests for him to work with 'I would prefer not to'. He refuses work but also refuses to leave the office. He is eventually moved to jail, where he refuses food and starves to death. While Bartleby's refusal ends with his death, it is the spirit of his refusal at the point of work that has proved inspirational. The feat of simply not doing something you're supposed to do, of

---

1 Ottessa Moshfegh, *My Year of Rest and Relaxation* (New York: Random House, 2018), p. 55.
2 https://harpersbazaar.com/culture/features/a12063822/emotional-labor-gender-equality/ (last accessed February 2021).

making a perfectly reasonable comment – *I would prefer not to* – is rendered unreasonable by the miasma of capitalist relations.

And yet the ambiguity of this refusal remains present. 'I would prefer not to' could refer to a particular act – in Bartleby's case, I would prefer not to copy out a particular letter, or to engage in the kind of effort required to look after myself – or it could refer to all manner of particular or general refusals. This ambiguity allows for the disavowal of the routine misery of contemporary work, indeed of contemporary life, without positing an alternative.[3] No wonder it has proved so popular – capitalism and its attendant cruelty is unpalatable, but alternatives remain beyond comprehension.

Perhaps a similar ambiguity can be found in the common internet expressions, 'I'm tired' and 'I can't even'. Both of these are invoked in opposition to something, but they leave open the possibility of what exactly the speaker is tired of or cannot deal with. As much as Bartleby's ambiguous refusal can act as a guide, a literary prompt, for the space that is opened up when someone says, or even merely imagines, that they will not do something, his is an escape that belongs to the world of male office workers in big cities in the nineteenth century. What would a Bartlebian act look like under contemporary capitalism?

For Hannah Murray, a lecturer in American Literature at the University of Liverpool, Ottessa Moshfegh's 2018 *My Year of Rest and Relaxation* can be read as a companion text to Melville's *Bartleby*. The novel has proved especially popular with millennial and Gen Z readers.[4] *My Year of Rest and Relaxation* is the story of an unnamed female protagonist, thin, young, WASPish and

---

3   See Slavoj Žižek, *The Parallax View* (Cambridge MA: MIT Press, 2006) for a discussion of this ambiguity.

4   See https://vice.com/en/article/jge4jg/want-to-read-more-during-the-lockdown-join-our-corona-book-club (last accessed December 2020).

highly privileged, who decides to take a year to sleep. More than just a modern-day Sleeping Beauty, her extended break – fuelled by dubiously obtained prescription drugs – became a simultaneously attractive and repellent escape for readers, a fantasy of refusal, not just of work but of all effort.

Murray tells me that 'like Bartleby, the narrator is rejecting work, status, friendship, the enjoyment of taking care of basic needs. The narrator's only friend, Reeva, is a devoted follower of all kinds of self-improvement guidance: 'partial to self-help books and workshops that usually combined some new dieting technique with professional development and romantic relationship skills, under the guise of teaching young women "how to live up to their full potential."'[5] The life and subjectivity that the protagonist is rejecting is the kind of achievement paradigm that neoliberalism enforces.

The protagonist, a self-described somnophile, had previously taken to napping while at work. While Bartleby offers non-compliance, *My Year of Rest and Relaxation* offers escapism, a temporary exit, for a very tired world. Amy Gaeta, a PhD candidate at the University of Wisconsin–Madison teaches the book to undergraduate students. She told me that her students

> tend to hate the narrator but love the novel itself . . . Some students still say they can relate to the character, but this disturbs them. Myself included here, tend to feel a bit of jealousy towards the protagonist: we work hard, and we are so tired too, why can't we rest for a year?

The drudgery, not just of formal work but also of endless, even unfinishable self-improvement, means that exhaustion is not

---

5   Moshfegh, *My Year of Rest and Relaxation*, p. 15.

acute but chronic. Gaeta thinks that this might be behind the book's success: 'it allows us to consider exhaustion as a universal condition'. It provokes us, she says, to 'consider what rest, relaxation, sleep, and waking even are' in a world in which our time is not our own; in Gaeta's words one in which 'everyone is exhausted and no one is sleeping.'

The openness and ambiguity of *My Year of Rest and Relaxation* might be appealing to those who are simply too exhausted to know what they would rather be doing. Similarly, the privileged cruelty of the book's main character is thrilling not only because it presents readers with the pleasure of second-hand transgression but because it strikes at the ways in which sociability is harnessed for profit. As Robin Craig, a doctoral researcher and fan of *My Year of Rest and Relaxation* told me:

> It tapped into my enjoyment of seeing things unravel, and it felt incredibly indulgent. Not just the escapism, but also the protagonist's haughtiness and judgement was something I often tamp down in myself to try and be a good person, but to see her enjoy it and even embrace it was delicious.

To take a year off requires significant wealth. It's the kind of thing that most people can only afford – with the help of state pensions and years of saving – at the end of their lives. It also requires someone else to carry out the work that provides the person who has temporarily excavated themselves from the labour market with anything they need to maintain themselves. In the case of *My Year of Rest and Relaxation* this work is undertaken by an immigrant workforce: the Egyptian men who run the bodega where the narrator picks up the coffees and ice creams, sustenance for her brief waking hours, the art prodigy, send-up of the New York art world, Ping Xi, to whom she hands over control of social reproductive functions of her life during the last months of her break. One person taking time off, stepping temporarily outside of wage labour, can require a network of often poorly paid workers to support them to meet their needs. As Hannah Murray puts it in reference to the New York of *My Year of Rest and Relaxation*, '[t]here is an entire infrastructure in the city of low income, largely non-white workers who do not have the material resources to stop working for months.'

This kind of retreat from work becomes itself a luxury commodity, dependent on further exploitation. While a break lasting as long as the one in Moshfegh's novel is not particularly common, corporate retreats that promise reflection, a restoration of meaning, re-balancing, and all other kinds of wellness hacks are common corporate perks. High fliers are given time off to focus on their side-projects and develop businesses that they find fulfilling and, one assumes, profitable. The very wealthy are able to step in and out of work as and when they choose, and find meaning and fulfilment rather than drudgery and alienation. Picking up the slack, picking up their laundry, driving them from corporate meeting to corporate retreat is an army of poor – usually women, and usually migrant – workers. Betty Friedan, liberal feminist of the American second wave, urged women to hire housekeepers to deal with the problem of time, to allow them to participate more fully in work, and to find themselves and meaning in so doing.[6] Gaining control over one's own time means, in a society like ours, that the work that we would do is dislodged rather than removed or transformed; it falls onto someone, typically another woman, with less social power, with less ability to refuse.

---

6   See Kathi Weeks, *The Problem with Work* (Durham, NC & London: Duke University Press, 2011), p. 173.

Who it is that fills the gap that the first refusal makes will depend on how social reproduction is carried out in that society. Consider the case of Henry David Thoreau. Thoreau, an American essayist, moved to a house in the woods, seeking to 'live deliberately, to front only the essential facts of life' against the murk of civilisation. His escape – a particularly American configuration of an older belief in and desire for escape from the corrupting effects of modern life – was made possible by his mother washing his clothes and bringing him food.

Family realism

In Joan Barfoot's 1978 novel, *Gaining Ground*, the natural environment again serves as the backdrop for fulfilment and pleasure absent in everyday life. Rather than the absence of effort, the novel takes a feminist autonomy generated through a return to an entirely effortful self-sufficiency in nature as its ambiguous idyll. The protagonist, Abra, leaves her husband and two children for a remote cabin in the woods. We can imagine her as a kind of female Thoreau, except rather than needing to be brought food, she makes her own, and makes a conscious choice not to make it for anyone else. She leaves behind a life of living for others, directed by clock-time which told her 'when to do each thing, waking, cooking, laundering, watching television, reading the newspaper',[7] for one directed by the rhythm of the seasons. Barfoot shows the lack of space for women to develop their own lives and selves because of a gendered distribution of domestic responsibility. Living for others – for children, for husbands – means a suspension of your own possibility.

7   Joan Barfoot, *Gaining Ground* (London: The Women's Press, 1992), p. 23.

And yet, while Abra finds pleasure in her escape, in the quiet life she builds for herself, the reader may struggle to understand her decision as anything other than a selfish one when she is confronted by the daughter, now nearly an adult, who she left behind all those years before. There is a cruelty that can come with claiming an isolated autonomy for yourself. The refusal of confining work, when that work is reproductive work, can pull the rug from those who would normally rely on it. The particular configuration of the family from which Abra is fleeing – the isolated, privileged, bourgeois family, with women as the almost exclusive providers of care – is a fundamentally constraining one. When her daughter finds her, years later, she feels her autonomy begin to recede, claiming that her daughter is 'chipping away at me'. That social and caring needs are typically met, indeed, often can only be met, within the family means that the emotional pull of familial relations at once necessitate and complicate her exit. In a similar vein, the poet Sylvia Plath described how:

My husband and child smiling out of the family photo;
Their smiles catch onto my skin, little smiling hooks.[8]

Gaining Ground pushes its readers to an uncomfortable position: if, as many might well do, we consider the family to be something that places an artificial, unfair, and unequal restriction on women's horizon of possibility, then leaving it – exiting, rather than attempting to reform that structure – might be justifiable. It is an uneasy proposal, made all the more uneasy by the knowledge that even having the choice of exit is a privilege. Even the nuclear family form, constraining and maddening as it

---

8 'Tulips', Sylvia Plath, *Collected Poems* (London: Faber, 1981), p. 160.

is, is itself something from which many are excluded. Migrant women, including the migrant women who clean the homes and care for the children of women in the Global North, are separated from their families by a violent and murderous border regime. And, as Black feminist theorists have pointed out, the lives of Black women have been historically marked by the violent denial of family life. And entering the world of work has never been a choice for working-class women.

An exit from the nuclear family is one that is rarely made. There have, however, been attempts to reconfigure the family, particularly by feminists and by queer activists, to imagine new ways of communal living, and structures of care. Of course, it's worth saying that the nuclear family is something of a historical aberration. The family has not been a constant through history; it is actually an unusual set up. Even when imagining the distant past, the family imagined is the nuclear family. A dad (who works) and a mum (who doesn't) and their two-and-a-bit kids. This naturalisation and de-historicisation of the family can be compared to capitalist realism – the insistence that there is no alternative to capitalism. Feminist scholar, Helen Hester, noting the formal similarities between these two dynamics, names the insistence on a particular kind of family life as the only possible 'family realism'. For a brief moment in the 60s and 70s, a crack appeared in family realism, or 'family chauvinism' as the American feminist Ellen Willis termed it. Many experimented with communal forms of living and developed new methods of child-raising. In some cases, these were informal and autonomous, with buildings squatted, becoming communes filled with multiple, multi-generation households, or shelters for women fleeing abuse. In others, demands were made for the state to fund new and better programmes. For example, the Working Women's Charter, a set of demands drawn up by women trade unionists in 1974, asked for free childcare.[9] Local chapters of the Women's Liberation Movement set up and defended community nurseries, which often began as squats.[10] Sometimes the demand was for the state to fund provisions like better childcare, but for those social goods to be run by the people who used them. These struggles for better working conditions both in and outside the home – led by social movements and by the labour movement – demanded an end to drudgery and an opening up of collective possibility; they were a struggle for less and better work.

Within a few decades, however, things had changed. I want to argue that the demand for less domestic drudgery didn't go away, but was instead replaced by individualised, neoliberal solutions. Rather than collective transformation, the reduction of women's domestic working time after the 1980s was premised on outsourcing and structural inequality.

Domestic life under family realism is architecturally individuated. Each family lives in its own separate home, within which many of the household functions for its members (with the important exceptions of schooling and care for the elderly) take place. This separation of public and private life reinforces the isolation of looking after children, particularly young children. The built environment of family realism did not escape the critical eye of the experimental spirit of the 60s and 70s. Fiona House, built in Leytonstone in 1972 by Nina West Homes, represents one attempt to reimagine domestic life. Designed for single parents, the flats looked out into a shared, spacious communal corridor, intended as a play area for young children.

---

9   See Sarah Stoller, 'Forging a Politics of Care: Theorizing Household Work in the British Women's Liberation Movement', *History Workshop Journal*, 85, 2018, pp. 96–118, p. 104.

10   Christine Wall, 'Sisterhood and Squatting in the 1970s: Feminism, Housing and Urban Change in Hackney' *History Workshop Journal*, 83, 2017, pp. 79–97, p. 83.

Intercoms connected the different flats so that neighbours could easily communicate with each other and could help to babysit each other's children. The scheme was limited in some ways. It was designed for young families, with room sizes unsuitable for older children, and it was intended as transitional housing, with families normally moving out after a year or so. While Fiona House was less capaciously transformative than some more immersive experiments in communal living, like experiments with communes and community-run nurseries, it did represent a break, albeit a temporary one for a fixed period in a household's lifespan, with the idea that each individual household is a totally separate unit. Even though this type of set up would offer benefits to many families, even ones appealing to the most hard-nosed business-supporting Tory – keeping childcare costs low, encouraging single mothers to get back to work – there now are very few of these schemes in existence.

Care chains

What replaced experiments in reducing the amount of time spent on domestic labour? The 80s saw not just a defeat of the left on multiple fronts, but also a return to family chauvinism from within the left.[11] The optimism of the 60s and 70s, buoyed by prosperity and the belief in a multiplicity of exciting alternatives, subsided. Women's interest in reducing the amount of time they spent on household tasks, however, did not. In fact, as more and more women continued to enter the job market, the demand for less time on the 'second shift' deepened. Some of this work was picked up by men. In 1965, the average American

---

11   See Sheila Rowbotham, 'Propaganda for domestic bliss did not only come from the right. "Left-wing" sociologists stood firm on the sanctity of the family' in *Woman's Consciousness, Man's World* (London: Pelican, 1977), p. 4.

woman spent 30 hours per week on housework; by 2010 the average was 16.2 hours. The average American man spent only 4.9 hours on housework in 1965, rising to 10 in 2010.[12] In the UK, the average woman of 1965 spent 3.65 hours on housework per day, compared to 24 minutes for the average man. In 2005, these figures were 2 hours and 0.8 hours, respectively.[13] Labour-saving devices and technologies – ready meals, frozen food and microwaves – have reduced the time tasks take, particularly when it comes to food preparation. The rise of takeaways also contributes, as have changing expectations for the formality of meals. Household tasks are frequently done by poorly paid workers, effectively outsourced. While live-in domestic servants are rare, having declined steeply after the First World War, periods of rising inequality, both domestically and globally, have led to upticks in the numbers of domestic workers. Access to cheap migrant labour has meant that a growing number of households outsource significant parts of their domestic labour. In 2004, 1 in 10 families in the UK hired domestic help of some kind, usually a nanny or a cleaner.[14] Only a decade later, one in three families reported having a cleaner. While wealthier families are more likely to pay someone to work in their homes, even one in four households on low incomes, those earning under £20,000 a year, hire regular domestic help of some kind.[15] An army of cleaners, nannies and au pairs provide cheap housework and childcare. About 700,000 people are employed in the cleaning

12 https://ncbi.nlm.nih.gov/pmc/articles/PMC4242525/ (last accessed December 2020).
13 https://demographic-research.org/volumes/vol35/16/35-16.pdf (last accessed December 2020).
14 http://news.bbc.co.uk/1/hi/uk/3824039.stm (last accessed December 2020).
15 https://dailymail.co.uk/news/article-3516617/One-three-families-pay-cleaner-35s-drive-trend-hiring-domestic-help.html (last accessed December 2020).

industry, which has an estimated turnover of £8.1 billion.[16] The number of people employed in the sector grew 10% between 2010 and 2015.[17]

Women – mainly middle-class women, but increasing numbers of working-class women too – are able to partially avoid participation in undesirable housework because of inequality in the UK and international inequality. This inequality establishes a reserve pool of cheap labour for care, domestic and other socially reproductive labour. Many of these workers are women. Some are older women, a group likely to be living in poverty.[18] In fact, around one fifth of workers in the cleaning sector are over 55.[19] Younger migrant workers of all genders do a huge amount of this work – delivering take-aways, cleaning private homes and public spaces, and care work for the sick and elderly. This pattern of migration is often described as a 'global care chain', whereby some combination of disinclination, state welfare cuts, or financial conditions that required both parents to work, set into motion, as Arlie Hochschild describes it, 'a series of personal links between people across the globe based on the paid or unpaid work of caring'.[20] A migrant woman fills the initial care gap, but this creates another in the country she has left. A paradigmatic example is '[a]n older daughter from a poor family who cares for her siblings while her mother works

16   https://equalityhumanrights.com/sites/default/files/the_invisible_workforce_full_report_08-08-14.pdf (last accessed December 2020).

17   http://bache.org.uk/resources/Pictures/1701%20BCC%20Industry%20Trends%20Report%20v1.3.pdf (last accessed December 2020).

18   https://theguardian.com/society/2019/aug/18/elderly-poverty-risen-fivefold-since-80s-pensions (last accessed December 2020).

19   http://bache.org.uk/resources/Pictures/1701%20BCC%20Industry%20Trends%20Report%20v1.3.pdf (last accessed December 2020).

20   Arlie Hochschild, 'Global Care Chains and Emotional Surplus Value' in Hutton, W. and Giddens, A. (eds) *On The Edge: Living with Global Capitalism*, (London: Jonathan Cape, 2000), p. 131.

as a nanny caring for the children of a migrating nanny who, in turn, cares for the child of a family in a rich country'.[21]

There are regular debates on the ethics of hiring cleaners. The ferocity of these pitched battles rarely applies to forms of domestic help that are seen as typically masculine. It's unusual to see anyone argue against hiring a gardener, for example. This is partly because of the especially exploitative nature of some domestic cleaning, premised as it is on extreme inequality. It's also because of the more intimate nature of the work, and the still-lingering assumption that women do enjoy or ought to enjoy housekeeping. During the early stages of the Covid-19 lockdown, prominent newspaper columnists defended their right to have someone clean their homes, even at significant risk to their health, on dubiously feminist grounds. Their argument was that without outsourcing domestic work it would be women who had to do the bulk of it.[22] We might wonder if their cleaners were not also women. When the journalist Owen Jones criticised the cavalier attitude that employers of cleaners were taking to workplace safety, he was accused of sexism. His accusers claimed to be fighting the idea that women have some natural duty or propensity to cleaning but the upshot of their argument was that it is fine for some *other* – i.e. poorer, usually migrant – women to pick up after them. Escaping the confines of the domestic feminine was their individual prerogative, not a shared horizon for all women.

A potentially more helpful set of debates can be found around the question of what those who employ cleaners – particularly those who consider themselves feminists – ought to pay them. Academic philosopher, Arianne Shahvisi, argues that if 'people

21   Ibid.

22   https://spectator.co.uk/article/the-underlying-sexism-of-the-conversation-about-cleaners-and-covid (last accessed December 2020).

outsource cleaning chiefly to save themselves time, they should presumably pay the cleaner for the cost of that time'.[23] As many people earn more than the average cleaner's wage, about £12 per hour, this would mean a significant increase in the hourly wage for cleaners.[24] As well as valuing their employee's time as equal to their own, Shahvisi argues for working hours across all sectors that leave all people with enough time for reproductive labour, with men being expected to do their fair share. These two goals are potentially helpful ones, but they do not extend beyond the horizon of the individual household. It seems important that we demand a reduction in the amount of reproductive work by increasing communal provisions. We might imagine canteens, as Rebecca May Johnson does in an essay on the nationalised 'British Restaurants' set up during the Second World War but allowed to decline in the peacetime years that followed.[25] These would be open to all, with decent working and eating conditions. We could imagine universal childcare, and support for collective ways of living that reduce the duplication of reproductive effort that the existing household model creates. When labour is made available cheaply because of the stickiness of low pay for women and the exploitation of migrant workers, there is a disincentive for the development of technological innovation: if it's cheaper to exploit someone than to come up with technology that reduces the time spent on that task or even obliterate it entirely. In fact, in interwar Britain, the development of domestic appliances and even the shift to the

23   https://mediadiversified.org/2018/09/07/pay-your-cleaner-what-you-earn-or-clean-up-yourself (last accessed December 2020).

24   https://inthewash.co.uk/cleaning/how-much-do-cleaners-charge-uk/ (last accessed December 2020).

25   https://dinnerdocument.com/2019/04/30/i-dream-of-canteens/ (last accessed December 2020).

use of electricity and gas in heating and cooking were delayed by the easy ability to hire servants.[26] Nowadays, household technologies are either expensive gimmickry or minor updates to existing machines, like digital rather than manual dials for washing machines. In fact, many new 'innovations' in domestic technology depend on the existence of a cheap pool of easily exploitable labour – like the American start-up making smart fridges that not only alert their owners when they've run out of milk, but raise an order for milk on Instacart, powered by poorly paid platform gig work.[27]

The question of whether hiring someone else to do your housework is feminist or not misses the point. Instead, the outsourcing of housework is a response to the recognition that lots of housework is miserable drudgery, as well as being likely to cause a multitude of musculoskeletal problems.

During the decades since the housework debates, women have refused housework in all kinds of ways. This refusal was initially experimental, looking to both communal and state forms of provision that would reduce the amount of time they spent on housework. New domestic practices spread, with men slowly taking on more housework. But during the reactionary backlash of the 1980s, these experiments either stalled or were defunded and outsourced. Nurseries, many of which were collectively set up and community-run, are now often run by huge multinational companies with poor working conditions, and 84% are privately run.[28] The picture for domestic work inside the home is no different. Rather than the socialisation of elements

---

26 Lucy Delap, *Knowing Their Place* (Oxford: Oxford University Press, 2011), p. 117.

27 https://vice.com/en_us/article/qjd8vq/gig-economy-now-making-workers-organize-groceries-in-rich-peoples-fridges (last accessed December 2020).

28 https://novaramedia.com/2020/09/17/big-business-is-muscling-in-on-the-uks-nursery-racket/ (last accessed December 2020).

of housework, a global market in service and care work, which has extreme global inequality as its precondition, has usurped attempts at remaking domestic life and work. Escape from work – whether paid or unpaid – leaves a gap. In a market society, this will usually be filled with a market response. Many individuals have tried to reduce the amount of work they do. But to transform work on a massive scale will require a different approach. Without building up robust, communal institutions, and shared prosperity of the kind that allowed the refusal of work in the 60s and 70s, resistance to work might yield a better life for the few individuals who are able to do it but will not lead to fairer outcomes for everyone.

Conclusion: Getting to work

The task of a successful socialist movement will be one of feeling and imagination quite as much as one of fact and organisation. – Raymond Williams

NO ONE WAY WORKS, it will take all of us
shoving at the thing from all sides
to bring it down. – Diana di Prima

What should we do about the problem of work? As I have shown in this book, the problem of work is not merely the issue of gaining fairer access to particular kinds of better jobs. This is because work under capitalism is arranged, *must be arranged*, in such a way that workers do not have control over their work. Work, for the vast majority of people, is not, as it promises to be, a viable means for self-expression, but an affront to freedom – something that eats up our lives. Because capitalism must always look for new frontiers and because profits must be secured, more and more people are brought more deeply into capitalist relations of production and their attendant relationships of power – between workers, their employers and the managers that surveil them.

Work under capitalism depends on and reproduces inequality. In societies with a widening gulf between the rich and the poor, like the contemporary UK, 'fairer' access to the remaining 'good' jobs ignores a fundamental fact: there will always be more people who lose out on 'good' jobs than there will be those lucky enough to win one. Addressing the problem of work must involve raising the floor rather than making it easier for a tiny number to puncture the ceiling. Increasing minimum standards at work and making sure that these standards are upheld and enforced, especially through a powerful and reinvigorated trade union movement, would make a significant difference to the lives of many people, protecting them from the worst excesses of capitalist work. This sort of change is unlikely to happen by the force of argument alone: it will require organising at deeper and deeper scales.

This levelling up would have a transformative impact – ending the timetable tyranny of zero-hours contracts, making it easier for workers to stand up against daily indignities, stymying the porous spread of work activity into non-work hours. It would not, however, do away with the fundamental issue of capitalist work: the relations of property and power that undergird it. Two existentially troubling concerns make the need to confront these relationships all the more urgent: climate crisis and the spectre of stagnating demand for labour, a situation in which there simply are fewer available jobs.

Despite knowing the horrific damage caused, companies and governments are still investing in fossil fuel infrastructure. They are preparing for coming decades of eking out profits while the planet burns around them. This is not merely a problem for now. That they are investing in fossil fuels at a greater rate than they are in renewable energy locks all of us into an extremely dangerous course of action for decades to come. When companies or governments invest in this infrastructure they will want to see a return on their investment, a return which forecloses a future for everyone. It's not enough for us to demand better minimum standards in work activity that is straightforwardly destroying the planet.

At the moment, the economy seems only capable of sputtering out jobs in low-paid service work. The effects that Covid-19 is likely to have on the finances of the service sector jeopardises even those jobs. Already we have seen youth (18–24) unemployment rise to 14.6% in November 2020, and over three quarters of a million jobs were lost between March and November 2020 alone. At the same time, unemployment remains understood as an individual failure of will rather than a political and structural problem. The coming years may well be characterised by crises of growing unemployment and underemployment, with fewer jobs available overall and fewer hours available in those jobs. Any solutions to the problem of capitalist work will have to address these two gathering storms.

The left in the UK operates in the shadow of two historic defeats. The first, and most recent, the 2015–19 attempt to hot-wire the immense power of the British state, through a social democratic party that was itself hostile to socialism. The second, and deeper still, was the destruction of the institutions of the organised working class during the last decades of the last century and continuing into this century. We remain in the wake of these two defeats. 'In the wake of' is so commonplace an idiom that we have lost sense of the violence and turbulence it might entail; a wake is the trail of disturbed, choppy water that a boat leaves behind it, or the destruction after a hurricane. The left – its organisations, its institutions, its members, all of us – are in the *wake* of these two defeats, thrown about in dangerous water, unable to grab hold of very much, trying to keep our heads above water.

This historical circumstance, this being-in-the-wake, makes theorising, strategising and taking stock all the more important and all the more difficult. These are not optimal conditions for action, but they are ones that necessitate action on a bigger and deeper scale than in previous historical circumstances. A first and a fundamental step is the task of rebuilding what has been dismantled or left to fray – the long hard work of re-founding and re-making the institutions of working-class power. Much of this might be building on the old lines, the exact foundations of what has come before, but some might look different, and will require experimentation.

While the underlying relations that make capitalism capitalism haven't changed, the ways in which those relations are lived have changed. This doesn't mean we should give up on the strategy of building the power of workers as a class, quite the opposite. But it does mean that potential entry points for this movement may have shifted. When the majority of workers are employed in the service sector, with its own pressure points different to those of industrial capital, new alliances and new tactics might need to be developed.

This doesn't mean an unorganised or scattered approach, but rather a tactical and strategic openness, looking to new possible directions, evaluating them critically, experimenting with them. A variety of solutions have been opposed to the problem of capitalist work: a jobs guarantee; worker ownership and/or worker management of firms; a reduction in working time; a universal basic income; universal basic services; full automation; and attempts to extricate the logic of work, or the work ethic from everyday life. I don't want to argue for a particular prescription, one clear, true path. Because of the centrality of the power relationship between employer and employee to what is harmful about work, I am most sympathetic to the transformation of work that would come from a transformation in ownership. But a hybrid combination of tactics might prove useful, not just for winning power or demands but for the process of denaturalising work.

Denaturalising makes visible that something is a historically contingent set of power-relations, rather than a 'natural', unchanging permanent state of affairs. Because capitalism, and, by extension, capitalist work, shapes our desires and our preferences so profoundly, a consciousness against capitalist work, a class consciousness, is something that needs to be developed, rather than something that appears automatically. Translating widespread frustration with individual jobs or individual bosses into frustration with the entire system of bosses and work requires this kind of consciousness.

One related route that seems promising for improving within the bounds of capitalism and challenging capitalist work is the radicalised demand for control over our time. This means time at work, free from micromanagement and the arbitrary tyranny of scheduling over zero-hours contracts and bogus self-employment. It also can extend to free time outside of the conventional workplace, for more time for other ways of being and living together. At the same time as this, building durable sites of communality, including democratically run public services that socialise elements of social reproduction, would offer ways of politicising time for everyday life, undoing the logic of capitalist work in everyday life. Such social institutions would mean that more free time isn't merely more 'free' consumer time, but free time replete with new possibilities for human cooperation and joy.

This conclusion's severe weather metaphors are not intended to make change seem impossible, but rather to allow us to look at the situation in which we find ourselves with clear eyes. We face deepening crises along with significant practical and theoretical challenges for the left as a movement, but what is at stake is not only control over our own lives, but over our collective destiny, our shared freedom and our shared joy. A future without the indignities, petty cruelties, exploitation and misery of capitalist work is possible, and it is one worth fighting for.

The Pluto Press Newsletter

Hello friend of Pluto!

Want to stay on top of the best radical books
we publish?

Then sign up to be the first to hear about our
new books, as well as special events,
podcasts and videos.

You'll also get 50% off your first order with us
when you sign up.

Come and join us!

Go to bit.ly/PlutoNewsletter